# AFTER LITTLE BIGHORN 1876 CAMPAIGN ROSTERS

*by*

## JAMES WILLERT

WARREN
A
VAN ESS
977

WARREN
A
VAN ESS
1977

JAMES WILLERT, PUBLISHER

LA MIRADA, CALIFORNIA

FIRST EDITION


c 1985 by James Willert



Library of Congress Catalog Card Number

International Standard Book Number 0-930798-07-4
(hard-cover edition)

International Standard Book Number 0-930798-08-2
(soft-cover edition)




Of this First Printing of the First
Edition of AFTER LITTLE BIG HORN:1876
CAMPAIGN ROSTERS, this is Copy No. 51h


Printed in the United States
of America

# INTRODUCTION

The purpose of AFTER LITTLE BIG HORN:1876 CAMPAIGN ROSTERS is that of a convenient volume of reference concerning the seventy-five companies of U.S. Infantry and Cavalry -- officers and enlisted men, and others -- who participated in the 1876 Indian War, following Custer's defeat at Little Big Horn (June 25-26). Nearly 4000 troops were in the field during this latter period. of the campaign, but there has never been an effort undertaken to identify all of them.

Names of casualties from the battles of Rosebud (June 17), and Little Big Horn, have not been included, since listings of these are already available in several published works. Neither have I included officers or men on detached service elsewhere, on leave, in confinement, etc. The men listed herein all served actively in the field during this summer's campaign; it is their identification this work concerns.

Several military commands joined the columns under Terry and Crook that summer:

Col. Elwell S. Otis, with six companies (230 men) of Twenty-Second Infantry, arrived at Terry's camp, along Yellowstone River, aboard the steamer Carroll on August 1. The following afternoon, Col. Nelson A. Miles, with six companies (346 men) of Fifth Infantry, arrived by way of steamers E.H. Durfee and Josephine -- and with this command, 150 recruits for the depleted Seventh Cavalry, sixty-four replacement horses, 80,000 rations, and two 3-inch Rodman guns.

Crook's Wyoming Column, encamped along Goose Creek, W.T., was strengthened July 13 with arrival of the Supply Train from Fort Fetterman, four companies (185 men) of Fourteenth Infantry, and one company (47 men) of Fourth Infantry (G) --and on August 3 with arrival of Col. Wesley Merritt, with ten companies (583 men) of Fifth Cavalry, 120 recruits (80 for the infantry), and 67 replacement horses.

This volume contains names of officers and enlisted men of the reinforcement commands, the commands originally in the field, and the dispositions of the recruits sent to fill casualty vacancies or strengthen companies. It will be noted that although the Seventh Cavalry Companies C,E,F,I and L (annihilated June 25) received assignments of recruits, dearth of sufficient cavalry horses obliged Terry to remount only Company C, and assign the other companies to duty as steamboat guards.

Thus, when Crook set forth August 5 down Tongue River, his force comprised 27 cos. of cavalry (1450 men), 10 of infantry (425), Shoshonee scouts (230), Ute scouts (20), citizens (30), and 350 pack mules carrying 150,000 rounds of ammunition, and 15 days' rations; and when Terry set forth August 8 up Rosebud, his force comprised 22 cos. of infantry (941 men), 12 of cavalry (732), Crow & Ree scouts (75), artillery (40), and 203 six-mule wagons transporting ammunition, and forage and rations for 25 days.

Names were obtained from Company rosters for August 31, 1876 (available on microfilm, Nat'l Archives, Washington,D.C.). Those difficult to read were cross-checked with June 30 or October 30 rosters before being set down. I hope errors are few, but if such are discovered, I would appreciate being informed so that subsequent editions may be made more accurate.

James Willert
April 1985

TABLE OF CONTENTS

Page

1    Steamer 'Far West' Crew & Complement
2    Dakota Column 'Headquarters' Command
3    Dakota Column Infantry Brigade Command
4    Dakota Column Cavalry Brigade Command
5    Seventh Infantry 'Headquarters' Command
6    Montana Column Quartermaster Department
7    Seventh Infantry 'Mounted Detachment'
     Seventh Infantry 'Gatling Battery Detachment'
8    Seventh Infantry : Company A
9    Seventh Infantry : Company B
10   Seventh Infantry : Company E
11   Seventh Infantry : Company H
12   Seventh Infantry : Company I
13   Seventh Infantry : Company K
14   Second Cavalry : Company F
15   Second Cavalry : Company G
16   Second Cavalry : Company H
17   Second Cavalry : Company L
18   Sixth Infantry : Company B
19   Seventeenth Infantry : Company C
20   Seventeenth Infantry : Company G
21   Twentieth Infantry 'Gatling Detachment'
22   Sixth Infantry : Company C
23   Sixth Infantry : Company D
24   Sixth Infantry : Company I
25   Sixth Infantry : Duty Escort on steamer 'Josephine'
26   Seventh Cavalry Detachment at Powder River Camp Supply
27   Seventh Cavalry Detachment at Powder River Camp Supply
28   Seventh Cavalry Command
29   Seventh Cavalry : Company A
30   Seventh Cavalry : Company B
31   Seventh Cavalry : Company C
32   Seventh Cavalry : Company D
33   Seventh Cavalry : Company E
34   Seventh Cavalry : Company F
35   Seventh Cavalry : Company G
36   Seventh Cavalry : Company H
37   Seventh Cavalry : Company I
38   Seventh Cavalry : Company K
39   Seventh Cavalry : Company L
40   Seventh Cavalry : Company M
41   Twenty-Second Infantry : Company E
42   Twenty-Second Infantry : Company F
43   Twenty-Second Infantry : Company G
44   Twenty-Second Infantry : Company H
45   Twenty-Second Infantry : Company I
46   Twenty-Second Infantry : Company K

TABLE OF CONTENTS

Page

47    Fifth Infantry Command
48    Fifth Infantry : Company B
49    Fifth Infantry : Company E
50    Fifth Infantry : Company F
51    Fifth Infantry : Company G
52    Fifth Infantry : Company H
53    Fifth Infantry : Company K

54    Wyoming Column 'Headquarters' Command
55    Fifth Cavalry Command
56    Fifth Cavalry : Company A
57    Fifth Cavalry : Company B
58    Fifth Cavalry : Company C
59    Fifth Cavalry : Company D
60    Fifth Cavalry : Company E
61    Fifth Cavalry : Company F
62    Fifth Cavalry : Company G
63    Fifth Cavalry : Company I
64    Fifth Cavalry : Company K
65    Fifth Cavalry : Company M
66    Second Cavalry Battalion Command
      Third Cavalry Battalion Command
67    Second Cavalry : Company A
68    Second Cavalry : Company B
69    Second Cavalry : Company D
70    Second Cavalry : Company E
71    Second Cavalry : Company I
72    Third Cavalry : Company A
73    Third Cavalry : Company B
74    Third Cavalry : Company C
75    Third Cavalry : Company D
76    Third Cavalry : Company E
77    Third Cavalry : Company F
78    Third Cavalry : Company G
79    Third Cavalry : Company I
80    Third Cavalry : Company L
81    Third Cavalry : Company M
82    Wyoming Column Infantry Battalion Command
83    Fourth Infantry : Company D
84    Fourth Infantry : Company F
85    Fourth Infantry : Company G
86    Ninth Infantry : Company C
87    Ninth Infantry : Company G
88    Ninth Infantry : Company H
89    Fourteenth Infantry : Company B
90    Fourteenth Infantry : Company C
91    Fourteenth Infantry : Company F
92    Fourteenth Infantry : Company I
93    The 'Sibley Scout' Detachment
94-121  INDEX

DAKOTA-MONTANA COLUMNS

|  | Off. | EM |
|---|---|---|
| FIFTH INFANTRY | 346 | |
| COMPANY B : | 3 | 63 |
| COMPANY E : | 1 | 58 |
| COMPANY F : | 3 | 58 |
| COMPANY G : | 2 | 61 |
| COMPANY H : | 2 | 58 |
| COMPANY K : | 2 | 65 |
|  | 13 | 363 |
| SIXTH INFANTRY | 8 | 165 |
| COMPANY B : | 2 | 37 |
| COMPANY C : | 2 | 36 |
| COMPANY D : | 2 | 32 |
| COMPANY I : | 1 | 35 |
|  | 7 | 140 |
| SEVENTH INFANTRY | 15 | 200 |
| COMPANY A : | 3 | 24 |
| COMPANY B : | 2 | 29 |
| COMPANY E : | 3 | 32 |
| COMPANY H : | 2 | 36 |
| COMPANY I : | 2 | 30 |
| COMPANY K : | 2 | 23 |
|  | 14 | 174 |
| SEVENTEENTH INFANTRY | 6 | 87 |
| COMPANY C : | 3 | 44 |
| COMPANY G : | 3 | 45 |
|  | 6 | 89 |
| TWENTY-SECOND INFANTRY | 17 | 212 |
| COMPANY E : | 1 | 34 |
| COMPANY F : | 2 | 41 |
| COMPANY G : | 3 | 40 |
| COMPANY H : | 2 | 35 |
| COMPANY I : | 3 | 31 |
| COMPANY K : | 3 | 35 |
|  | 14 | 216 |
| TWENTIETH INFANTRY GATLING GUN DETACH. : | 2 | 23 |

|  | Off. | EM |
|---|---|---|
| SECOND CAVALRY | 10 | 182 |
| COMPANY F : | 2 | 47 |
| COMPANY G : | 3 | 34 |
| COMPANY H : | 2 | 41 |
| COMPANY L : | 3 | 40 |
|  | 10 | 162 |
| SEVENTH CAVALRY | 16 | 545 |
| COMPANY A : | 1 | 38 |
| COMPANY B : | 1 | 61 |
| COMPANY C : | 1 | 42 |
| COMPANY D : | 2 | 57 |
| COMPANY E : | 1 | 44 |
| COMPANY F : | 1 | 44 |
| COMPANY G : | 3 | 45 |
| COMPANY H : | 2 | 39 |
| COMPANY I : | 1 | 37 |
| COMPANY K : | 1 | 53 |
| COMPANY L : | 1 | 42 |
| COMPANY M : | 1 | 41 |
|  | 17 | 543 |

TOTALS

|  | | |
|---|---|---|
| 5TH INF. | 13 | 363 |
| 6TH INF. | 7 | 140 |
| 7TH INF. | 14 | 174 |
| 17TH INF. | 6 | 89 |
| 22ND INF. | 14 | 216 |
|  | 54 | 982 |
| 2ND CAV. | 10 | 162 |
| 7TH CAV. | 17 | 543 |
|  | 27 | 705 |

Note: Sub-head numbers indicate Terry's estimate on August 8th of OFF & EM.

WYOMING COLUMN

| | Off. | EM | | | Off. | EM |
|---|---|---|---|---|---|---|
| **SECOND CAVALRY** | | | | **FOURTH INFANTRY** | | |
| COMPANY A : | 3 | 55 | | COMPANY D : | 2 | 52 |
| COMPANY B : | 1 | 58 | | COMPANY F : | 2 | 49 |
| COMPANY D : | 2 | 59 | | COMPANY G : | 2 | 45 |
| COMPANY E : | 2 | 52 | | | 6 | 146 |
| COMPANY I : | 2 | 41 | | | | |
| | 10 | 265 | | **NINTH INFANTRY** | | |
| | | | | COMPANY C : | 3 | 45 |
| **THIRD CAVALRY** | | | | COMPANY G : | 2 | 46 |
| | | | | COMPANY H : | 3 | 46 |
| COMPANY A : | 2 | 56 | | | 8 | 137 |
| COMPANY B : | 2 | 61 | | | | |
| COMPANY C : | 2 | 56 | | **FOURTEENTH INFANTRY** | | |
| COMPANY D : | 2 | 47 | | | | |
| COMPANY E : | 2 | 59 | | COMPANY B : | 2 | 45 |
| COMPANY F : | 2 | 49 | | COMPANY C : | 2 | 46 |
| COMPANY G : | 1 | 55 | | COMPANY F : | 2 | 41 |
| COMPANY I : | 2 | 42 | | COMPANY I : | 2 | 45 |
| COMPANY L : | 2 | 44 | | | 8 | 177 |
| COMPANY M : | 3 | 50 | | | | |
| | 20 | 519 | | | | |
| | | | | **TOTALS** | | |
| **FIFTH CAVALRY** | | | | | | |
| | | | | 2ND CAV. | 10 | 265 |
| COMPANY A : | 3 | 57 | | 3RD CAV. | 20 | 519 |
| COMPANY B : | 1 | 56 | | 5TH CAV. | 18 | 565 |
| COMPANY C : | 2 | 61 | | | 48 | 1349 |
| COMPANY D : | 2 | 63 | | | | |
| COMPANY E : | 2 | 59 | | | | |
| COMPANY F : | 2 | 59 | | 4TH INF. | 6 | 146 |
| COMPANY G : | 2 | 54 | | 9TH INF. | 8 | 137 |
| COMPANY I : | 1 | 52 | | 14TH INF. | 8 | 177 |
| COMPANY K : | 1 | 56 | | | 22 | 460 |
| COMPANY M : | 2 | 48 | | | | |
| | 18 | 565 | | | | |

Note: The figure differences given in the Introduction and those
listed above merely indicate that when Crook moved out August 5th.
some of those in the above list remained behind with the Wagon Train
encampment on Goose Creek, W.T.

Drawing by Warren A. Van Ess

1985

WARREN
A
VAN ESS

STEAMER 'FAR WEST' CREW & COMPLEMENT

CAPT. GRANT MARCH (Skipper)
DAVID CAMPBELL, Pilot
BEN THOMPSON, First Mate
GEORGE FOULK, Chief Engineer
JOHN HARDY, Second Engineer
WALTER BURLEIGH, Clerk


(ESCORT)


COMPANY B, SIXTH INFANTRY (CAPT. STEPHEN BAKER, Comd'g), until
29 July, when General Alfred Terry replaced this command with
Sgt. Michael Caddle (Co.I, 7th Cav.) and 16 dismounted troopers
of the Seventh Cavalry.

The TWENTIETH INFANTRY DETACHMENT on board were the following:

Sgt. Peter E. Monaghan (Co.D or Co.I)
Cpl. Thomas Tully (Co.G)
Pvt. Phillip W. Devereux (Co.B or Co.D)
Pvt. James J. McGirr (Co.G)
Pvt. Charles Birns (Co.G or Co.I)
Pvt. John Mains (Co.I)


(COMPLEMENT)


1st Sgt. James E. Wilson, Corps. of Engrs.
Pvt. Thomas Culligan, Corps. of Engrs.
Pvt.        Goslin, Corps. of Engrs.
James Sipes, Barber
James Coleman, Trader
William 'Billy' W. Carland
    (son of 1st Lt. John Carland (Co.B, 6th Inf.)
Alfred W. Dale, Hospital Steward
Joseph Rhinehart, Hospital Steward
James Boles
Reuben Reilly
John Johnson
Mr.  Hall
    (and probably others)

## HEADQUARTERS COMMAND

BRIG.GEN. ALFRED HOWE TERRY (Comd'g)
CAPT. EDWARD WORTHINGTON SMITH (Co.G, 18th Inf.), Acting Assistant
    Adjutant General
CAPT. ROBERT PATTERSON HUGHES (Co.E, 3rd Cav.), Aide-de-Camp
1ST LT. EUGENE BEAUHARNAIS GIBBS (Co.C, 6th Inf.), Aide-de-Camp
CAPT. OTHO ERNEST MICHAELIS (Ordnance Corps), Chf. Ord. Officer
1ST LT. HENRY JAMES NOWLAN (7th Cav.), Act'g Assist. Quartermaster
1ST LT. EDWARD MAGUIRE (Corps. of Engineers), Chf. Engr. Officer
2ND LT. HENRY PERRINE WALKER (Co.G, 17th Inf.), Assist. Engr.
2ND LT. RICHARD EDWARD THOMPSON (Co.K, 6th Inf.), Assist. Commissary
    of Subsistence

DR.(CAPT.) JOHN WINFIELD WILLIAMS, Chief of Medical Dept.
DR. HOLMES O. PAULDING, Surgeon (MONTANA COLUMN)
DR. LOUIS TESSON, Acting Surgeon (FIFTH INFANTRY)
DR. HENRY PORTER, Surgeon (SEVENTH CAVALRY)
DR. P.H. HARVEY, Assistant Surgeon
DR. J.P. KIMBALL, Assistant Surgeon
DR. TAYLOR (Marcus E. or Blair D.), Assistant Surgeon
DR. BARBOUR
DR. ELBERT J. CLARK, Medical Director with Cavalry Battalion
DR. ISAIAH H. ASHTON, Medical Director for Infantry Battalion

MATTHEW CARROLL, In Charge of 'Diamond R' Wagon Train (E.G.Maclay
    & Co.) with Montana Column.

## SCOUTS

George Herendeen                George W. Morgan
'Muggins' Taylor                Vic Smith
Luther 'Yellowstone' Kelly      Zed H. Daniels
Edward Begley ('Jimmy from Cork')   Charles 'Sandy' R. Morris
Thomas LeForge (Montana Column)     William 'Billy' Cross
William E.'Yank' Brockmeyer     Robert Jackson
William 'Billy' Jackson         John Williamson
George Mulligan                 'Scout' Baker

## CORRESPONDENTS

James J. O'Kelly [New York Herald]
James William 'Phocion' Howard [New York Times; New York Daily
    Tribune; Chicago Tribune]
Charles Sanford Diehl [Chicago Times]

INFANTRY BRIGADE : COMMAND

COL.(BVT.BRIG.GEN.) JOHN GIBBON (Comd'g)

(RIGHT WING)

COL.(BVT.BRIG.GEN.) NELSON A. MILES (Comd'g)

FIFTH INFANTRY (Col. Nelson A. Miles)

| | |
|---|---|
| COMPANY B | CAPT. ANDREW S. BENNETT |
| COMPANY E | 2ND LT. JAMES W. POPE |
| COMPANY F | CAPT. SIMON SNYDER |
| COMPANY G | CAPT. SAMUEL OVENSHINE |
| COMPANY H | 1ST LT. EDMUND RICE |
| COMPANY K | 1ST LT. MASON CARTER |

SIXTH INFANTRY (Major Orlando Hurley Moore)

| | |
|---|---|
| COMPANY C | CAPT. JAMES W. POWELL |
| COMPANY D | CAPT. DANIEL H. MURDOCK |
| COMPANY I | 2ND LT. GEORGE B. WALKER |

(LEFT WING)

COL. ELWELL STEPHEN OTIS (Comd'g)

TWENTY-SECOND INFANTRY (Col. Elwell Stephen Otis)

| | |
|---|---|
| COMPANY E | CAPT. CHARLES J. DICKEY |
| COMPANY F | CAPT. ARCHIBALD H. GOODLOE |
| COMPANY G | CAPT. CHARLES W. MINER |
| COMPANY H | CAPT. DEWITT C. POOLE |
| COMPANY I | CAPT. FRANCIS CLARKE |
| COMPANY K | CAPT. MOTT HOOTEN |

SEVENTH INFANTRY (Col. John Gibbon)

| | |
|---|---|
| COMPANY A | CAPT. WILLIAM LOGAN |
| COMPANY B | CAPT. THADDEUS S. KIRTLAND |
| COMPANY E | CAPT. WALTER CLIFFORD |
| COMPANY H | CAPT. HENRY BLANCHARD FREEMAN |
| COMPANY I | 1ST LT. WILLIAM L. ENGLISH |
| COMPANY K | CAPT. JAMES M.J. SANNO |

## CAVALRY BRIGADE : COMMAND

### SEVENTH CAVALRY

MAJOR MARCUS ALBERT RENO (Comd'g)


FIRST BATTALION : CAPT. FREDERICK WILLIAM BENTEEN (Comd'g)

| | |
|---|---|
| COMPANY C | 1ST LT. EDWARD GUSTAVE MATHEY |
| COMPANY G | 1ST LT. FRANCIS MARION GIBSON |
| COMPANY H | 1ST LT. ERNEST ALBERT GARLINGTON |
| COMPANY M | CAPT. THOMAS HENRY FRENCH |

SECOND BATTALION : CAPT. THOMAS BENTON WEIR (Comd'g)

| | |
|---|---|
| COMPANY A | CAPT. MYLES MOYLAN |
| COMPANY B | CAPT. THOMAS MOWER McDOUGALL |
| COMPANY K | 1ST LT. EDWARD SETTLE GODFREY |
| COMPANY D | CAPT. THOMAS BENTON WEIR |


### SECOND CAVALRY

MAJOR JAMES SANKS BRISBIN (Comd'g)

| | |
|---|---|
| COMPANY F | 2ND LT. CHARLES FRANCIS ROE |
| COMPANY G | CAPT. JAMES NICHOLS WHEELAN |
| COMPANY H | CAPT. EDWARD BALL |
| COMPANY L | 1ST LT. SAMUEL TODD HAMILTON |


ARTILLERY DETACHMENT : 1ST LT. CHARLES AUSTIN COOLIDGE (Comd'g)

"...a battery of ten-pound rifles and one 12-pounder." Several 3-inch Rodman guns, Napoleon brass cannon, and Gatling guns.

TWENTIETH INFANTRY GATLING GUN DETACHMENT : 2ND LT. WILLIAM HALE LOW, JR. (Comd'g)

HEADQUARTERS GUARD : MAJOR ORLANDO HURLEY MOORE (Comd'g)

(Companies' C,D,I, Sixth Infantry, of Col.Miles' Right Wing)

'FORT BEANS' COMMAND : CAPT. LOUIS H. SANGER (Co.G, 17th Inf.) (Comd'g) : "...a breastwork....Three Gatling guns....About 160 men...." 'Fort Beans' existed from 7 Aug. to 21 Aug. on site of Terry's Camp, north bank of Yellowstone, opposite Rosebud Creek.

## MONTANA COMMAND HEADQUARTERS

COL.(BVT.BRIG.GEN.) JOHN GIBBON (Comd'g)

1ST LT. LEVI FRANK BURNETT, 7th Inf. Adjutant
1ST LT. JOSHUA WEST JACOBS, 7th Inf. Quartermaster
1ST LT. JAMES HOWARD BRADLEY (Co.B, 7th Inf.)
        (Chief of Mounted Detachment of Scouts)
2ND LT. CHARLES ALBERT WOODRUFF (Co.K, 7th Inf.)
        (Comd'g Artillery)
2ND LT. EDWARD JOHN McCLERNAND (Co.G, 2nd Cav.)
        (Acting Engineering Officer)
2ND LT. CHARLES BREWSTER SCHOFIELD (Co.L, 2nd Cav.)
        (2nd Cav.Battalion Adjutant)


### (Enlisted)


Sgt. James E. Wilson (Engineers)
Sgt. Charles Becker (Engineers)(Co.D)


### PRIVATES


Joseph Weis, (Co.D), 1st Clerk
Carl Pilts (HQ) Pioneer Party
Robert F. Williams (Co.D), hosp. attendant
James Bovard (Co.F, 2nd Cav.), hosp. attendant
Mathew F. Canning (Co.H, 2nd Cav.), hosp. attendant

QUARTERMASTER DEPT. (FORT PEASE)

1ST LT. JOSHUA WEST JACOBS (QUARTERMASTER,7th Inf.)

SEVENTH INFANTRY

Sgt. James E. Moran (Co.K)          Cpl. Christian Sipfler (Co.A)
Sgt. Lewis G. Einbaum (Co.D)        Cpl. William Baker (Co.G)
Artif. Joseph Klewitz (Co.A)        Artif. Charles W. Fannin (Co.K)

PRIVATES

(SEVENTH INFANTRY)                  (SECOND CAVALRY)

Charles Alberts (Co.A)              George H. Barnes (Co.F)
John O. Bennett (Co.B)              John J. Clarkins (Co.G)
William Carson (Co.I)               Herbert O. Evans (Co.G)
Holmes L. Coon (Co.G)               Edward J. Hamilton (Co.G)*
James Doyle (Co.A)                  Joseph Igglesden (Co.H)
Peter W. Frost (Co.F)               Nicholas James (Co.H)
Charles Heinze (Co.G)               John Keegan (Co.G)
Frank McCollum (Co.F)               Jackson Kennedy (Co.G)
Frederick Meyer (Co.K)              Philip Low (Co.L)
William Moore (Co.A)                William H. Power (Co.G)
Frank Morton (Co.G)                 George C. Smith (Co.G)
George Rogers (Co.K)                Charles Stevens (Co.L)
Joseph C. Sinsil (Co.B)             Robert Sturm (Co.L)
George von Thianich (Co.H)          John Tavlane (Co.G)
James A. Watson (Co.B)              Charles Webber (Co.G)
Peter Young (Co.H)                  Henry Young (Co.G)

* Identified 4 July as a deserter, James Miles, Pvt.,Company M,
  Seventh Cavalry.

SEVENTH INFANTRY : MOUNTED DETACHMENT

1ST LT. JAMES HOWARD BRADLEY (Co.B) (Comd'g)

Sgt. Joseph L. Farrell (Co.G)          Cpl. James D. Abbott

PRIVATES

James E. Goodwin (Co.A)          William MacIntosh (Co.K)
Henry S. Groff (Co.H)            John Madden (Co.B)
David Heaton (Co.K)              Henry Rice (Co.H)
Robert M. Isgrigg (Co.G)         William Roller (Co.I)
Albert Kifer (Co.B)              Martin Sullivan (Co.G)
                James Walsh (Co.A)

SEVENTH INFANTRY : GATLING BATTERY

2ND LT. CHARLES ALBERT WOODRUFF (Co.K) (Comd'g)

Cpl. James Randall (Co.A)          Cpl. Frederick Stortz (Co.K)

PRIVATES

August W. Bender (Co.K)          Frank Murphy (Co.K)
Lummen W. Hoffman (Co.K)         Morris Roche (Co.A)

SEVENTH INFANTRY : COMPANY A

CAPT. WILLIAM LOGAN (Comd'g)
1ST LT. CHARLES AUSTIN COOLIDGE
2ND LT. FRANCIS WOODBRIDGE
(joined 17 August at Powder River confluence)

1st Sgt. John Rafferty

Sgt. Samuel Plant                           Cpl. Paul Daniels
Sgt. Richard B. Dickinson                   Cpl. Adolph Heinzman
Sgt. George C. Meysel (ill at Ft. Pease)    Musc. John McLennon

PRIVATES

Lorenzo D. Brown                            John C. Martin
George W. Cullom                            Joseph Smith
James Drew                                  John B. Smith
Thomas Harrington                           Edward Stumpf
Levi Heider                                 William Walter
George Leher                                Patrick Sullivan
James C. Lehmer                             James Collins

(Temporarily Attached)

William H. Aubrey (Pvt. Co.G)
John J. Conner (Pvt. Co.G)
Isaac H. Spayd (Pvt. Co.G)

SEVENTH INFANTRY : COMPANY B


CAPT. THADDEUS SANFORD KIRTLAND (Comd'g)
2ND LT. CHARLES AUSTIN BOOTH


1st Sgt. John Cashman

Sgt. William Wolchert                    Cpl. George Jabowing
Cpl. Henry Smith                         Cpl. Thomas Baiggo

Musc. Philip Reid


PRIVATES


John Baaer                               William Ickler
Herbert Clark                            James Knox
Patrick Coakly                           John Miller
Alfred DeGroot                           Edward Mulcahy
Augustus W. Ford                         Edgar W. Parker
Frank Geiger                             Edward Poetling
Frederick Groshan                        Martin Reap
Frank E. Hastings                        Louis Striber
William Hinkler                          Sylvester Waltz

August Weber


(Temporarily Attached)


Frank McHugh (Pvt. Co.G)
James Norton (Pvt. Co.G)
Edward Welsh (Pvt. Co.G)

SEVENTH INFANTRY : COMPANY E


CAPT. WALTER CLIFFORD (Comd'g)
2ND LT. GEORGE SHAEFFER YOUNG
1ST LT. WILLIAM ISAAC REED
(joined 17 August at Powder River confluence)


1st Sgt. Peter T.R. Van Ardenne

| | |
|---|---|
| Sgt. James Bell | Cpl. John C. Clark |
| Sgt. Daniel Dommitt | Cpl. William D. Bendell |
| Cpl. Collomb Spalding | Musc. George C. Beary |
| Cpl. William Wright | Musc. John Rafferty |


PRIVATES


| | |
|---|---|
| Charles A. Barker | John Miller |
| James Bell | Vincent McKenna |
| John Burns | James McKibben |
| Matthew Butterly | William Noonan |
| John Duane | Thomas O'Malley |
| Matthias Efferts | August Raw |
| William Evans | Walter S. Robertson |
| William Funk | William H. Sanders |
| William Hensley | Thomas Scott |
| Francis Honicker | Benjamin F. Stewart |
| Lewis G. Hubbard | Samuel Wallace |

George W. Wood


(Temporarily Attached)


Riley R. Lane (Sgt. Co.D)
John Howard (Pvt. Co.D)

## SEVENTH INFANTRY : COMPANY H

CAPT. HENRY BLANCHARD FREEMAN (Comd'g)
2ND LT. FREDERICK MONROE HILL KENDRICK

1st Sgt. George G. Howard

Sgt. Charles R. Hill                    Cpl. Eugene Navarra
Sgt. George Stein                       Cpl. Patrick Rudden
Sgt. Edward M. Ferguson                 Cpl. James Costello
Cpl. William Moran                      Musc. Francis Rein

### PRIVATES

Joseph Barkman                          George Matthews
Joseph Biddle                           Martin Miller
William Bolts                           Michael Partridge
John H. Buskirk                         James Reader
Robert Copely                           George Rivers
Thomas Curran                           Albert Ross
Patrick J. Finigan                      Henry Scott
Augustus Freiberg                       Archy T. Segman
Eugene Grant                            Charles Walters
Elijah Hall                             William West
Albert H. Jones                         George F. Woodard
Peter Lorentzen                         William H. Woodhouse
Thomas Martin                           Frank Wolf

### (Temporarily Attached)

William D. Mathews (Pvt. Co.G)

SEVENTH INFANTRY : COMPANY I

1ST LT. WILLIAM LEWIS ENGLISH (Comd'g)
2ND LT. ALFRED BAINBRIDGE JOHNSON

1st Sgt. Thomas H. Wilson

Sgt. Milden H. Wilson                  Cpl. Charles Bishop
Sgt. Michael Rigney (ill on 'Far West')  Cpl. George A. Wolfe
Sgt. Michael Hogan                     Cpl. John L. Reynolds
Sgt. Patrick Bosquill                  Cpl. Richard M. Cunliffe
  (dischgd 16 July on'Josephine')

PRIVATES

John Bane                        Peter Moan
James Bell                       Nicholas Murphy
Thomas Collins                   Richard Orrington
Lewis Chaplin                    Thomas Ralph
Patrick Fallon                   Peter Scanlon
Thomas Frost                     Walter Selden (dischgd 16
Henry W. Gray                       July on'Josephine')
Charles J. Keegan                Calvin Smith
  (dischgd 16 July on'Josephine')  Peter Tenni
William Louett                   William Thompson
  (dischgd 16 July on'Josephine')  James Wilhight
Edward Linehau                   Thomas Wilkinson

## SEVENTH INFANTRY : COMPANY K

CAPT. JAMES MADISON JOHNSON SANNO (Comd'g)
2ND LT. CHARLES ALBERT WOODRUFF
(Battalion Adjutant, Seventh Infantry,with HQ)


1st Sgt. Walter E. Garlock

Sgt. Thomas F. Stanford          Sgt. Henry E. Schreiner
Sgt. Lewis Hines (ill at Ft. Pease)    (Co.B. Acting Commissary
Sgt. William J. Wilson              Sgt.,attached to Co.K)
Musc. Herman Wendling            Artif. John Kleis


### PRIVATES

Howard Clark                     Robert Marlow
Orison C. Cochran                James McFarland
Peter H. Conniff                 Noah G. Pomeroy
Joseph Gallagher                 Joseph Sanford
Philo O. Hurlburt (ill at Ft. Pease)   William Simon
Charles Keating                  Michael Stritten


(Temporarily Attached)


Michael Fogarty (Pvt. Co.G)
John Meier (Pvt. Co.G)


(Confined in the Field 17 April)


Jacob Goldberg

SECOND CAVALRY : COMPANY F


2ND LT. CHARLES FRANCIS ROE (Comd'g)
1ST LT. WILLIAM PHILO CLARKE (joined Column 17 Aug.
   at Powder R. & appt. Aide to Crook 21 Aug.'76 by
   Terry's Order.)


1st Sgt. Alexander Anderson

Sgt. John R. Nelson              Cpl. Edward G. Granville
Sgt. Thomas Wallace              Cpl. E. Dwight Chapman
Sgt. William Leipler             Trp. William C. Osmer
Sgt. Richard Davis               Blksm. Joseph Baker
Sgt. John H. Sarven              Far. William J. Cleeland
Sad. Thomas Jones                Pvt. Charles Leslie (mail
Cpl. Ausburn B. Conklin (Mail escort        escort to Fort Ellis)
       to Fort Ellis,M.T.)       Pvt. Johan Youk (mail escort
                                            to Fort Ellis)


PRIVATES


Frederick Allen                  David Melvill
William Burke                    John G. Moore
Benjamin Betts                   John J. O'Flynn
Thomas Carroll                   John O'Sullivan
Robert H. Cowen                  Adolf Puryear
Michael Cowley                   William S. Parker
John E. Duggan                   Daniel C. Starr
James Farrell                    George Sibbeske
Thomas Graham                    George Shuless
Frank Glackewsky                 William F. Somers
Edward Harrington                Edward Seibert
Charles E. Hall                  Thomas Turnholt
John W. Jones                    Henry Watson
Christie Kaiser                  Joseph Waller
Charles A. Lauthammer            George S. Wall
John McLaughlin                  William H. White

## SECOND CAVALRY : COMPANY G

CAPT. JAMES NICHOLS WHEELAN (Comd'g)
1ST LT. GUSTAVUS CHEENY DOANE
2ND LT. EDWARD JOHN MCCLERNAND
(Act'g Engr. Officer for Montana Column)


1st Sgt. George E. Barnaby

| | |
|---|---|
| Sgt. George W. Prentice | Cpl. Frederick E. Server |
| Sgt. Andrews Peffer | Cpl. Christian Allspach |
| Sgt. George Perry | Cpl. Patrick Cigan |
| Sgt. John Ruth | Cpl. Kermit G. Nail |
| Trp. Christian Leitz | Trp. Wheeler H. Polk |
| Blksm. Thomas Hinton | Sad. Robert Somers |


### PRIVATES

| | |
|---|---|
| Fowler R. Applegate | John Irving |
| John F. Atkinson | Joseph Kroll |
| Herbert Bixby | Michael Kearney |
| James A. Chamberlain | Walter Lookstedt |
| John Dale | Francis Long |
| Wiley D. Dean | Charles Mallis |
| John Dugan | Michael McCaffery |
| John Fitzgerald | William G. Osborn |
| Morris H. Huth | James Rotchford |
| Thomas K. Collins | Watson P. Stone |

Thomas White

SECOND CAVALRY : COMPANY H


CAPT. EDWARD BALL (Comd'g)
1ST LT. JAMES GEORGE 'JOHNNY' MCADAMS


1st Sgt. John R. Elkins

Sgt. Clifford Pearson          Cpl. Francis Stewart
Sgt. John McCabe (ill at Ft. Pease)   Cpl. Charles Grillon
Sgt. Frank Whitney             Cpl. Andrew Kennedy
Sgt. Thomas Kelly              Far. Edward Wells
Blksm. Charles Murray          Sad. James Beverly
                Trp. Thomas Carney (ill at Ft. Pease)


PRIVATES


James Adams                    John Kern
William Benson                 George T. Lawlor
John Brown                     William Miller
John Carroll                   Thomas McDonald
James Carroll                  Victor McKelery
John Clark                     George S. Meyers
Joseph H. Davis                Francis Phillips
James R. Dipp                  Frank Ruland
Thomas Duffy                   John Reardon
Joel S. Flanigan               Henry Schargenstein
Thomas B. Gilmore              Frank Walters
Henry E. Gray (ill at Ft. Pease)   Richard Walsh
Thomas S. Hoover               John B. Warren
George F. Kane                 William Wherstedt

SECOND CAVALRY : COMPANY L


CAPT. LEWIS THOMPSON (Comd'g)
1ST LT. SAMUEL TODD HAMILTON
2ND LT. CHARLES BREWSTER SCHOFIELD
 (Battalion Adjutant : Second Cavalry)


1st Sgt. Henry Wilkins

| | |
|---|---|
| Sgt. Emil Plum | Cpl. Charles Egert |
| Sgt. Charles E. Weston | Cpl. William Thompson |
| Sgt. Edward Page | Cpl. Martin Shannon |
| Sgt. John F. McBlain | Trp. Harry B. Melville |
| Sgt. John F. Prutting | Trp. Samuel A. Glass |
| Far. Ansil Riden | Sad. John Cox |


PRIVATES


| | |
|---|---|
| Konrad Bubenheim | David Murphy |
| John C. Chase | John O'Conner |
| George Cook | James Ryan |
| John W. Davis | Maxim Robideau |
| John Flanigan | James Sanderson |
| Daniel Gallagher | John Thompson |
| Samuel Hendrickson | Arthur Ward |
| William H. Jones | Joseph Whalen |
| William Jenkins | Edward Williams |
| Michael Kelly | William Wilson |
| Jean J. Malcolm | John Winkle |
| Jacob Mauren | David H. Winters |
| Fred M. Munn | Wade H. Young |

Charles R. Davis

SIXTH INFANTRY : COMPANY B


CAPT. STEPHEN BAKER (Comd'g)
1ST LT. JOHN CARLAND


1st Sgt. Thomas Farrell

Sgt. Hugh Kernan                          Cpl. Peter Engelhardt
Sgt. William Brinkman                     Musc. James Sharlett
Cpl. William R. Mooney                    Musc. Daniel DeLany


PRIVATES


James Armstrong                   Barney Kamphouse
Charles Birach                    John Kistler
Albert E. Brown                   William Langton
William Buckley                   James Martin
James Cameron                     Michael McCarthy
James Clark                       Patrick F. McCarthy
William Costigan                  Michael G. Minchin
Patrick N. Crowley                James Murray
John Dark                         Thomas Nolan
John Duffy                        John O'Conners
Spencer Edwards                   John Sarratt
John Falardo                      William Scott
Patrick Fitzimmons                Conrad Sieffert
Julius B. Fleming                 Edward T. Spring
Robert F. Jones                   George Withrow


(Temporarily attached to COMPANY B, SIXTH INFANTRY, from the
TWENTIETH INFANTRY GATLING GUN DETACHMENT, 29 MAY 1876)


Sgt. Peter E. Monaghan (Co.I)         Cpl. Thomas Tully (Co.G)
Pvt. Philip N. Devereaux (Co.B)       Pvt. James McGirr (Co.G)
Pvt. Charles Birns (Co.I)             Pvt. John Mains (Co.I)

SEVENTEENTH INFANTRY : COMPANY C


CAPT. MALCOLM MCARTHUR (Comd'g)
1ST LT. FRANK DILLON GARRETTY
2ND LT. JAMES DALLAS NICKERSON


Sgt. Charles Smith              Cpl. Patrick Mulcahy
Sgt. Eugene Snow                Cpl. James Dignon
Sgt. Joseph Marchand            Cpl. Carl Kohlepp


PRIVATES


Frank F. Bang                   James McElroy
Charles Becker                  William McLain
Sanford F. Brown                Louis P. Milligan
John H. Cummins                 Charles Odeu
John Curtis                     John H. Perkins
Leonard Deitz                   John J. Phillips
Richard Fowler                  Thomas Plunkett
Charles Fox                     Eli Prescott
Thomas W. Graham                Thomas W. Rance
Joseph Greenwald                Frank Shepler
James Gruver                    Alex F. Smith
William Harris                  John F. Spalding
Joseph Heuser                   John Speirs
John Hunter                     Robert Sproul
James Kelly                     Charles H. Stewart
Martin Kruger                   Frank H. Thomas
George McAlvey                  Hugh C. Thompson
Caspar Strohm                   John L. Waldo

Andrew Johnson
(attendant to Dr. Isaiah Ashton)


(Confined in the Field)


William H. Crosby

SEVENTEENTH INFANTRY : COMPANY G


CAPT. LOUIS H. SANGER (Comd'g)
1ST LT. JOSIAH CHANCE (Depot Quartermaster)
2ND LT. HENRY PERRINE WALKER


1st Sgt. William Bolton

Sgt. George F.W. Miller          Cpl. John Stanley
Sgt. William Mayer               Cpl. David Street
Sgt. Frank E. Osgood             Cpl. John McCarthy
Sgt. James Hewitt                Cpl. Thomas Parnell
Musc. Michael Crowley            Artif. James Brierly


PRIVATES


Charles F. Almon                 Edward B. McCarthy
Darian W. Batterall              John McCarthy
Charles Beckman                  Charles Miller (1st)
Herman Binkhoff                  Charles Miller (2nd)
Frederick G. Bond                Charles Muller
William Butler                   William Myers
John Casey                       Fulton A. Nichols
Samuel Cling                     Louis R. Nieschang
Owen P. Duffy                    Terence O'Brien
George Ferrers                   John Petit
Martin Gannon                    William Ritchart
Henry Keeler                     Thomas Rogers
George Kellerman                 Walter Seamon
John Lyons                       Francis A. Steele
Francis Marriaggi                Philip Trotvine
John D. Massingale               Maurice Ward
Albert Davis                     John Whitford

TWENTIETH INFANTRY : GATLING GUN DETACHMENT


2ND LT. WILLIAM HALE LOW, JR. (Co.C) (Comd'g)
2ND LT. FRANK XAVIER KINZIE (Co.F)


Sgt. Hugh Hynds (Co.B)           Cpl. Jacob W. Crawford (Co.B)
Sgt. Lafayette Davis (Co.C)      Cpl. Peter G. Burdeff (Co.F)
Sgt. Edward Alexander (Co.I)     Cpl. Thomas F. Oldsworth (Co.H)


## PRIVATES


Rufus Henderson (Co.B)       James Gordon (Co.F)
Thomas F. Boen (Co.C)        Thomas Powers (Co.F)
William A. Ellis (Co.C)      William Robinson (Co.F)
John McCormick (Co.C)        William G. Smith (Co.F)
Edward McDonald (Co.C)       James Gomely (Co.H)
Edward Lowell (Co.D)         Napoleon Miller (Co.H)
George Rivers (Co.D)         John Pangburn (Co.H)
Neal Devlin (Co.F)           James Shields (Co.H)
              William Kelly (Co.I)

SIXTH INFANTRY : COMPANY C


CAPT. JAMES WILLIAM POWELL, JR. (Comd'g)
2ND LT. BERNARD ALBERT BYRNE (Acting Commissary &
                        Quartermaster for Battalion)


1st Sgt. Edward B. Hanson

| | |
|---|---|
| Sgt. Michael Morris | Cpl. Charles Randolph |
| Sgt. James Dooley | Cpl. Charles Muessigbrodt |
| Sgt. Frederick Seaver | Cpl. George W. Crans |
| Artif. Hans Storm | Artif. Emanuel L. Hoffman |

Musc. Michael Foley


PRIVATES


| | |
|---|---|
| Robert D. Atcheson | Daniel Maloney |
| James Bisbing | Thomas Mathews |
| Joseph Broderick | Joseph McElevey |
| William H. Brown | George Monach |
| William H. Cecil | Patrick Murphy |
| Warner Colwell | August Reis |
| Daniel Corcoran | William F. Sagle |
| William Feaha | Charles Simon |
| William A. Hall | Frederick W. Smith |
| Henry Hamilton | Henry J. Smith |
| Joseph Jacobs | Henry C. Soltneidel |
| John Kenny | Richard Thornton |

William H. Wiggins


(Confined in the Field)


Jeremiah Kieley (since 28 June)

SIXTH INFANTRY : COMPANY D

CAPT. DANIEL HAMILTON MURDOCK (Comd'g)
1ST LT. FREDERICK WILLIAM THIBAUT
(Comd'g Escort on steamer 'Josephine')

1st Sgt. John J. Bowman

Sgt. William G. Gayle            Cpl. James P. Foreaker
Sgt. Joseph Fox                  Cpl. James W. Rodgers
Cpl. Samuel McLaughlin           Cpl. Charles F. Lawson
            Trp. William Copestick

PRIVATES

Elmore Bradley              Martin McGowan
Thomas Clark                John W. Michley
Michael Connell             Jacob Pippher
Daniel Deegan               Martin Ramey
Ole Halverson               Webster Rednor
Angelo Howard               David Robinson
George Howard               Wilmot P. Sanford
Henry Howard                Thomas R. Smiley
Frank Hughes                Levi A. Stone
Albert Hummell              Samuel E. Teeters
John Maley                  Aaron T. Weierbach
            James Winn

(Confined in the Field)

James Costigan

SIXTH INFANTRY : COMPANY I

2ND LT. GEORGE BRANTON WALKER (Comd'g)

1st Sgt. Oscar W. Litchfield

Sgt. George H. Love                    Cpl. Samuel Middaugh
Sgt. Dennis Donavan                    Cpl. George McKee
Sgt. Charles Roberts                   Cpl. Charles H. Adams
Sgt. George Walker                     Musc. Louis Wahler
  (Acting Sgt.Major for Battalion)

PRIVATES

William S. Beaver               Hugh McLaughlin
Patrick Boyle                   Peter O'Donnell
Michael Buggle                  James E. Redd
Peter F. Clarison               Dennis Ring
John Craig                      Thomas Sanders
John H. Drusselmeir             August Schomberg
Thomas Enright                  Benjamin F. Shortis
Sylvester Fitzpatrick           Jacob Smith
John  F. Frank                  John Smith
Charles Johnson                 Charlie Stierle
Griffith Jones                  Joseph Thalon
John Leonard                    John Walsh
William Magee                   John C. Warner

SIXTH INFANTRY : DUTY ESCORT ON STEAMER, 'JOSEPHINE'

1ST LT. FREDERICK WILLIAM THIBAUT (Co.D) (Comd'g)


Sgt. John Scott (Co.C)                    Sgt. Alexander Wyley (Co.D)
              Cpl. William S. Doyle (Co.C)


PRIVATES


John H. Cassidy (Co.C)          Thomas Gibney (Co.D)
Edward Felber (Co.C)            William J. Mulhern (Co.D)
Louis Kamer (Co.C)              William M. Palmer (Co.D)
Charles Schwab (Co.C)           John Dunlap (Co.I)
Julius Simonson (Co.C)          Amos W. Littlejohn (Co.I)
James Daly (Co.D)               William A. Sartain (Co.I)
              John J. Sttuka (Co.I)

## SEVENTH CAVALRY : AT POWDER RIVER CAMP SUPPLY

QM Sgt. Thomas Causby (7th Cav.HQ)
Sad. Sgt. John G. Tritten (7th Cav.HQ)
Vet. Surgeon C.A. Stein (7th Cav.HQ)
Com. Sgt. Charles Brown (7th Cav. HQ)

### SEVENTH CAVALRY BAND

Chf. Musc. Felix V. Vinatieri

### PRIVATES

Otto Arndt                                          Peter Eisenberger
Conrad Baumbach                                     Jacob Emerich
Benjamin Beck                                       Julius Griesner
Edmond Burlis                                       Julius Jungsbluth
Andrew Carter                                       Bernard O'Neill
Joseph Carroll                                      George Rudolph
                        Thomas Sherbon

### SEVENTH CAVALRY

### COMPANY A

August Bockerman (Ft.Lincoln,7 Aug.)        John Ragsdale
Benjamin Burdick (Powder River 13 Aug.)        (Ill,Ft.Lincoln,6 Aug.)

### COMPANY B

Jacob W. Doll                                       John L. Littlefield
John J. Keefe                                       Bernard McGurn
                        Thomas O'Brien

### COMPANY C

William Kane (Ill, Ft.Lincoln)              Julius Van Arnim
Charles M. Orr                              Wag. Frank Starck (DS,
Blksm. John Fitzgerald (DS,Powder River)        Powder River)

SEVENTH CAVALRY : AT POWDER RIVER CAMP SUPPLY

### COMPANY D

Stephen Cowley                                      Uriah S. Lewis
                  Gustav Harlfinger (dischgd 5 Aug.)

### COMPANY E

William W. Chapman

### COMPANY F

### COMPANY G

Charles Barney                             George K. Henderson
Martin Kilfoyle                            (On steamer,Yellowstone)

### COMPANY I

Far. John Rivers

### COMPANY K

Jacob Horner                               Emil Taube
Wag. Albert Whytenfield                    William A. Van Pelt

### COMPANY L

                  Cpl. John Minden (Or Nunan?)
Frederick Lepper                           Michael Keegan
                  Max Hoehn

### COMPANY M

James McCormick                            Wag. Joseph Ricketts

## SEVENTH CAVALRY : COMMAND ROSTER

MAJOR MARCUS ALBERT RENO (Comd'g)
2ND LT. GEORGE DANIEL WALLACE (Co.G), Adjutant
2ND LT. WINFIELD SCOTT EDGERLY (Co.D), Quartermaster

COMPANY A        CAPT. MYLES MOYLAN

COMPANY B        CAPT. THOMAS MOWER McDOUGALL

COMPANY C        1ST LT. EDWARD GUSTAVE MATHEY (Temp. Comd.)

COMPANY D        CAPT. THOMAS BENTON WEIR (Comd'g 2nd Bn.:Cos.A,B,K,D)

COMPANY E        1ST LT. CHARLES CAMILUS DERUDIO

COMPANY F        2ND LT. EDWIN PHILIP ECKERSON

COMPANY G        1ST LT. FRANK (FRANCIS) MARION GIBSON
                     (Comd'g to 27 August)
                 1ST LT. ERNEST ALBERT GARLINGTON
                     (Comd'g after 27 August)

COMPANY H        CAPT. FREDERICK WILLIAM BENTEEN
                     (Comd'g 1st Battalion, Companies C,G,H,M)
                 1ST LT. FRANK (FRANCIS) MARION GIBSON
                     (Comd'g after 27 August)
                 1ST LT. ERNEST ALBERT GARLINGTON
                     (Comd'g Co.H)

COMPANY I        2ND LT. CHARLES ALBERT VARNUM

COMPANY K        1ST LT. EDWARD SETTLE GODFREY

COMPANY L        1ST LT. LUTHER RECTOR HARE

COMPANY M        CAPT. THOMAS HENRY FRENCH

    Due to a lack of horses, many of the new recruits to the
Seventh Cavalry were assigned to guard duty aboard the several
steamboats, and/or the temporary breatworks known as 'Fort Beans'.
    Consequently, on 7 August, General Orders No.18 provided
mounts for only Company C, and organized the eight companies into
two battalions:
        ]st Battalion, Capt. Benteen comd'g : Cos. H,G,C,M
        2nd Battalion, Capt. Weir comd'g    : Cos. A,B,D,K

## SEVENTH CAVALRY : COMPANY A

### CAPT. MYLES MOYLAN (Comd'g)

Act'g 1st Sgt. George M. McDermott

| | |
|---|---|
| Sgt. Samuel Alcott | Cpl. Richard W. Corwin |
| Sgt. Henry Fehler | Cpl. Otto Durselew |
| Sgt. Ferdinand A. Culbertson | Far. John Bringes |
| Sgt. John Thomas Easley | Sad. John Muering |
| Cpl. Stanislaus Roy | Blksm. Andrew Hamilton |
| Trp. William G. Hardy (Chf.Trp.HQ) | Trp. David McVeigh |

### PRIVATES

| | |
|---|---|
| Charles Aller | John W. Franklin(packer) |
| Neil Bancroft | John M. Gilbert |
| Louis Baumgartner | David W. Harris |
| Wilbur F. Blair | Stanton Hook(Ill,28 Aug.) |
| Thomas Blake | Samuel Johnson |
| George Bott(Ill,hosp.25 Aug.) | Emil O. Jonson |
| James F. Bartholf (R) | William McClurg |
| Henry Brown (R) | William D. Nugent |
| John E. Cleveland (R) | George H. Proctor |
| William Collins (R) | Thomas Seayers |
| Andrew Conner | Anton Siebelder |
| Cornelius Cowley(Ill,hosp.3 Aug.) | William O. Taylor(Ill,6Aug) |

Howard H. Weaver

(R) Recruits joined Column 2 August.

SEVENTH CAVALRY : COMPANY B


CAPT. THOMAS MOWER McDOUGALL (Comd'g)


1st Sgt. James Hill

Sgt. Rufus D, Hutchinson            Cpl. Adam Wetzel
Sgt. Thomas Murray                  Cpl. Charles Cunningham
Sgt. Peter Gannon                   Trp. James Kelly
Sgt. Benjamin Criswell              Trp. John Connell *
Sgt. Daniel Carroll                 Blksm. John Crump
Cpl. James Dougherty                Far. James E. Moore (dischgd.
                  Sad. John E. Bailey      28 Aug.)


PRIVATES


Peter O. Barry(DS:HQ)               John Gray
James F. Barsantee                  Ferdinand Klaweitter
William Boam                        William Martin
Ansgarius Boren(abs.:Rosebud)       John McCabe
George Brainard(Orderly:HQ)         Terence McLaughlin
James ·Brown                        William McMasters
Charles Burns                       William E. Morrow
James Callan                        Thomas O'Brien(abs.:Rosebud)
William Caldwell(Ill,'Far West')    John O'Neill
Charles A. Campbell                 James Pym
John J. Carry                       George F. Randall
Thomas Carmody                      Stephen L. Ryan
Henry Criswell(Ill,'Far West')      Hiram W. Sager
Frank Clark                         Daniel Shea
Thomas W. Coleman                   Patrick Simons
Michael Crowe                       Philip Spinner
Patrick Crowley                     Edward Stout
William H. Davenport                James Thomas
  (Ill,'Far West')                  Henry L. Tinkham
Louis DeTourriel                    William Trumble
Augustus L. DeVoto                  Richard A. Wallace **
William Frank                       Aaron Woods (Co.cook)
Fred H. Gehrmann                    Charles A. Werner (R)(2 Aug.)
                  Edwin B. Wight (Ill,'Far West')


* Accidentally shot himself in heel 21 May;DS,Powder R.15 June.Rejoin-
  ed after Battle of Little Big Horn.
** Drowned while going on picket nr. mouth Big Horn, 25 July.

SEVENTH CAVALRY : COMPANY C

1ST LT. EDWARD GUSTAVE MATHEY (Temp. Comd'g)


Sgt. Daniel Knipe
Sgt. Richard P. Hanley *
Cpl. Charles A. Crandall
Blksm. William Markham (DS,HQ 3 Aug.)

Wag. Frank Starck(DS,Powder River)
Blksm. John Fitzgerald (DS, Powder River)


PRIVATES


Charles H. Bischoff
Joseph Bouger (R)
Patrick Brady (R)
William Brandle
John Brennan
Herbert Cook (R)
John Corcoran
Henry Dannenfelsor(R)
Nicholas Dodds (R)
Frank Ellison (R)
Morris Farrer
Isaac Fowler
John Gates (R)
Fulton Green (R)
John B. Hird (R)
Charles H. Holland (R)
William Hoppe (R)
Leander R. Jester

John Jordan
James Lawler (R)
John Mahoney
John J. Martin (R)
William B. Martin (R)
Charles Mauch (R)
Thomas McCreedy
Frank Mulligan (R)
Martin Mullin
Ottocar Nitsche
Charles N. Oakley (R)
Frank A. Palmer (R)
John G. Roett (R)
Eli Shaw (R)
John Stevens (R)
Robert Walker
James Watson
Adolf von Soffine (R)
  (DS, HQ, 3 Aug.)


(R) Recruits joined Column 2 August.
* At risk of life, Hanley caught ammunition-carrying pack mule headed
  for Indians' position during Little Big Horn Battle 25 June 1876.
  Awarded Medal of Honor 5 October 1878.

SEVENTH CAVALRY : COMPANY D

CAPT. THOMAS BENTON WEIR (Comd'g)
2ND LT. WINFIELD SCOTT EDGERLY
(Appointed Quartermaster, 7th Cav.)

1st Sgt. Michael Martin

Sgt. Thomas Morton
Sgt. Thomas W. Harrison
   (dischgd. 5 Aug.)
Sgt. James Flanagan
Sgt. Thomas Russell
Cpl. Albert Cunningham
Cpl. George W. Wylie
Trp. Aloys Bohner

Sgt. Charles H. Houghtaling
   (appt. 1 July)
Cpl. Henry Holden (appt. 1 July)
Cpl. John H. Welch (appt. 1 July)
Blksm. Frederick Deitline
Far. Henry G. Smith
   (appt. 1 Aug.)
Sad. John Meyers

PRIVATES

James H. Alberts
John B. Ascough
Abram B. Brant
Thomas Conlan
Thomas Cox
George Dann
David E. Dawsey
John J. Fay
Harvey A. Fox(dischgd 24 July)
John Fox
Joseph Green
Curtis Hall
William Hardden
James Harris
William M. Harris(dischgd 5 Aug.)
John Hayer
Jacob Hetler
George Horn
George Hunt
James Hurd (dischgd 5 Aug.)
James Kavanagh

John Keller
Fremont Kipp
John Kretchmer
Jesse Kuehl
David Manning
William A. Marshall
Patrick McDonnell (abs.:Ill)
John Meadwell(dischgd 26 July)
William Muellor
William O'Mann
John Quinn
William J. Randall
Elwyn S. Reid
William Sadler
Charles Sanders
George D. Scott(dischgd 5 Aug.)
John S. Sims
William E. Smith
Thomas W. Stivers(dischgd 5 Aug.)
Frank Tolan
James Wynn

George H. Vreeland (R)

(R) Recruit joined Column 2 August.

SEVENTH CAVALRY : COMPANY E

1ST LT. CHARLES CAMILUS DERUDIO (Comd'g)


Sgt. Lawrence Murphy                    Far. Able B. Spencer
Blksm. Henry Miller                     Sad. William Shields


PRIVATES


Harry Abbotts                           John McKenna
Frank Berwald                           Charles Napoleon (R)(DS*)
Latrobe Bromwell                        Henry O'Mahon (R)(DS*)
Stephen O. Buskirk (R)                  Charles D. Orr (R)(DS*)
John W. Burkett (R)(DS*)                Francis O'Toole (DS:HQ)
Michael F. Carey (R)(DS*)               Christopher Pandtle(DS:hosp.)
Joseph H. Cornell (R)(DS*)              Patrick Powers (R)(DS*)
William F. Craile (R)(DS*)              Charles M. Robertson (R)(DS*)
Fernando Davidson (R)(DS*)              Garrison L. Stoy (R)(DS*)
John Davis (R)(DS*)                     Henry W. Stoy (R)(DS*)
Daniel C. Hefferman (R)(DS*)            Henry A. Stone (R)(DS*)
Charles Huebner (R)(DS*)                John Walsh (R)(DS*)
Peter Jones (R)(DS*)                    Frederick Waltz (R)(DS*)
John G. Kimm                            Patrick Waters (R)(DS*)
George King (R)(DS*)                    Frank H. West (R)(DS*)
Henry Lange                             Henry Wilkins (R)(DS*)
Henry Martyn (R)(DS*)                   Charles Zimmer (R)(DS*)
Daniel McGlone (R)(DS*)                 Eugene Egan (R)
Michael McGlone (R)(DS*)                George Foerstall (R)
                    William Reese (DS 11 Aug.)


(Transfer)

William H. Chapman (Pvt.).Transferred from Co.B to Co.E.
                    DS since 24 Aug.


(R) Recruits joined Column 2 August.
(DS*) Due to lack of horses, these recruits assigned to guard duty
      on the steamboats, and/or 'Fort Beans'.

SEVENTH CAVALRY : COMPANY F

2ND LT. GEORGE DANIEL WALLACE (Temp. Comd'g,
        until appointed Adjutant, 7th Cav.)
2ND LT. EDWIN PHILIP ECKERSON (Comd'g)
        (joined Column 2 August)


Sgt. William A. Curtiss                    Cpl. Edward Clyde
                  Sad. Claus Schleiper


PRIVATES


John Baker (R)(DS*)                 Dennis Lynch (dischgd.6 Aug.)
Hiram E. Brown(teamster,HQ)         Bernard Lyons
Ulrich Burke (R)(DS*)               Daniel McCarthy (R)(DS*)
James Butler (DS:hosp.)             Frank Meyers
George H. Chamberlin (R)(DS*)       Adam Mikler (R)(DS)
Gustav Cooney (R)(DS*)              Joseph Milton (DS)
Edward Davern                       James Mundlay (R)(DS*)
Thomas Dunn (R)(DS)                 Nicholas Muster (R)(DS*)
William Eades(mechanic,HQ)          Leander Nelon (R)(DS*)
   (dischgd.6 Aug.)                 William H. Paris (R)(DS*)
Thomas J. Finnegan                  Edwin H. Pickard
Charles Goff (R)                    Albert Pilcher (HQ)
William J. Gregg                    John Quinlan (R)(DS*)
Francis Hegner(laborer,HQ)          Michael Reilley
Harry B. Hill (R)(DS*)              James M. Rooney
Anton Holpe (R)                     Herbert Roper (R)(DS*)
Frank Howard                        Paul Schleiforth(Commissary,
Frank Hunter (dischgd.6 Aug.)                         HQ)
Matthew Joyce (R)                   Frederick Shutte
Clarence Kimber (R)(DS*)            Peter Sparks (R)(DS*)
Meig Lefler                         John W. Sweeney
                  Thomas Walsh (DS*)


(R) Recruits joined Column 2 August.
(DS*) Due to lack of horses, these recruits and dismounted troopers
      assigned to guard duty on the steamboats, and/or 'Fort Beans'.

## SEVENTH CAVALRY : COMPANY G

1ST LT. FRANK (FRANCIS) MARION GIBSON (Comd'g to 27 Aug.)
1ST LT. ERNEST ALBERT GARLINGTON (Comd'g after 27 Aug.)
2ND LT. GEORGE DANIEL WALLACE (Appointed Adjutant,7th Cav.)


Sgt. Alexander Brown
Sgt. Orlaus Northeg
Sgt. John E. Hammon
    (promoted fr.Cpl.25 June)
Sgt. James Akers
    (promoted fr.Cpl.25 June)
Cpl. John W. Wallace (Appt.25 June)

Cpl. Henry Brinkerhoff
    (Promoted 25 June)
Cpl. Melancthon H. Cressey
    (Promoted 25 June)
Cpl. George Loyd (DS:hosp.)
    (Promoted 25 June)
Blksm. Walter O. Taylor

### PRIVATES

James P. Boyle
Edmond Dwyer
Theodore W. Goldin
Thomas Graham
William S. Gray
Edward Grayson
Frank Geist
John Hackett
Benjamin Johnston
Jacob Katzenmaier
Joseph Laden
John Lattman (DS:Ordnance Wag.)
Frank Lauper
Samuel McCormick
John McDonnell
James McDunough (R)(DS*)
John McEagan
Hugh McGonigle (DS:Ord.Wag.)

Edmond T. McKay
John McKee
John Morrison
Thomas O'Neill
Henry Petring
John A. Reed (DS)
Eldorado I. Robb
Robert Rowland
John Shanahan (DS:Co.G Wagon)
John R. Small
James H. Smith (R)
Thomas Sorden (R)(DS*)
George W. Stephens
Thomas Stevenson (DS)
Daniel Sullivan
Joseph Tulo
Markus Weiss
Pasavan Williamson (Deserted
    while on DS 7 July)


(R) Recruits joined Column 2 August.
(DS*) Due to lack of horses, these recruits assigned to guard duty
    on the steamer 'Far West'.

SEVENTH CAVALRY : COMPANY H


CAPT. FREDERICK WILLIAM BENTEEN (Comd'g 1st Battalion,
            Companies C,G,H.M, 7th Cav.)
1ST LT. FRANK (FRANCIS) MARION GIBSON (Comd'g Co.G,
            on Temporary Assignment)
1ST LT. ERNEST ALBERT GARLINGTON (Comd'g Co.H)
            (Joined Command 2 August)


                1st Sgt. Joseph McCurry (appt.Sgt.Maj.HQ,1 Aug.)
Sgt. Patrick Conelly                    Trp. William Ramell
Sgt. Mathew Maroney                     Trp. John Martin(DS 28 Aug)
Sgt. Thomas McLaughlin(dischgd 6 Aug.)  Cpl. Daniel Nealon
Sgt. George Geiger                      Sad. Otto Voit
            Blksm. Henry W.B. Mecklin


PRIVATES


Jacob Adams                          George Kelly
Charles E. Avrey                     James Kelly
Frederick Bender (R)                 Thomas Lawhorn
Henry P. Bishley                     Thomas McDermott
Richard Bucher (R)                   James McNamara
William Channell (Deserted*)         David McWilliams (Ill,
John Day                                Powder River:dischgd
George W. Dewey                         29 August)
Edward Diamond (DS)                  Edler Nees (Deserted*)
George W. Glease                     John Nagles (R)
Timothy Haley                        Joshua S. Nicholas
Henry Haack                          John S. Pinkston
Thomas Hughes                        William O. Ryan
Charles W. Hood                      William C. Williams
John Hunt (dischgd. 6 Aug.)          Charles C. Windolph
            Aloyse L. Walter (DS 14 Aug.)


(R) Recruits joined Column 2 August.
(Deserted*) Channell and Nees deserted 26 July from camp near mouth
    of Big Horn, but were apprehended 28 July.Confined, Fort Lincoln.

SEVENTH CAVALRY : COMPANY I

2ND LT. CHARLES ALBERT VARNUM (Comd'g)


Sgt. Milton DeLacy               Sgt. Michael Caddle
Sgt. George Gaffney              Sgt. James P. McNally
Sgt. Robert L. Murphy               (appt. 1 July)
          Cpl. William Cordello (appt. 10 Aug.)(R)
               (Ill, hosp.,Ft. Lincoln)


### PRIVATES


Franz C. Braun                   Patrick Lynch
Robert Bryant (R)                Andrew McAllister (R)
Peter Burns (R)                  William McFeeters (R)
Edward B. Cromley (R)(DS*)       John McShane
George W. Dinsmore (R)           John Minnick (R)
George Dixon (R)                 Frederick Myers
Stephen Elwood (R)               James Myls (R)
John Goggin (R)                  Charles Overton (R)
Gabriel Geesbacher               Eugene Owens (R) (DS,Artil-
John C. Herr (R)                    lery, Oct., 1876)
Frederick Hagenbach (R)          Eugene H. Penney (R)
Henry P. Jones                   Charles Ramsey (R)
Francis Johnson                  George Raston (R)
Gustav Korn                      Jacob Traubman (R)(14 Aug.)
Charles A. Kron (R)              Frank Thomas (R)(DS*)
John Laparr (R)(DS*)             George H. Tresh (R)(DS*)


(R) Recruits joined Column 2 August.
(DS*) Due to lack of horses, some recruits assigned to guard duty
      on the steamboats, and/or 'Fort Beans'.

## SEVENTH CAVALRY : COMPANY K

### 1ST LT. EDWARD SETTLE GODFREY (Comd'g)

1st Sgt. Louis Rott

| | |
|---|---|
| Sgt. Andrew Frederick | Cpl. William W. Lasley |
| Sgt. Jeremiah Campbell | Trp. George B. Penwell |
| Sgt. John Rafter | Trp. Christian Schlafer |
| Sgt. George Hose (appt.12 July) | Cpl. Edmund H. Burke |
| Cpl. John Nolan | Blksm. Daniel Lyons |
| Cpl. Henry Murray | Far. Cecil R. Leverett(R) |
| Sad. Christian Boissen | (appt. 1 August) |

### PRIVATES

| | |
|---|---|
| Charles Ackerman(Godfrey's cook) | Alonzo Jennys |
| Jacob Bauer | Wilson McConnell |
| James Blair | Martin McCue |
| George Blunt(dischgd.5 Aug.) | Michael Murphy(dischgd.5 Aug.) |
| Cornelius Bresnahan (DS) | Thomas Murphy |
| Joseph Brown (DS) | Michael Ragan |
| Charles Burgdorf | Henry W. Raichel |
| Charles Burkhardt | Michael Reilly |
| (dischgd. 5 Aug.) | Jonathan Robers |
| Charles Chesterwood(Regt.HQ) | Francis Roth |
| Patrick Coakley (DS) | John Shauer |
| John C. Creighton (DS) | John Schwerer |
| Michael Delaney * | August Siefert |
| John Donahue | Frederick Smith |
| John Foley (DS) | John R. Steintker (reduced |
| William Gibbs | from Farrier 1 August) |
| Thomas A. Gordon (DS) | Ernest Wasmus |
| Thomas Green | William Whitlow |
| Andrew Holahan | George A. Wilson |
| Walter Hoyt ** | Henry Witt |

Charles Stapleton (R) (12 July)

(R) Recruit joined Column 1 August.
* Accidental gunshot wound 7 July. Transferred to hosp.
** Dislocated finger 14 July.

## SEVENTH CAVALRY : COMPANY L

### 1ST LT. LUTHER RECTOR HARE (Comd'g)

1st Sgt. Henry Bender

Sgt. John Mullen                                    Cpl. George Zimmerman (R)
Sgt. Peter E. Rose          Cpl. William Logue          (appt. 2 Aug.)

### PRIVATES

William G. Abrams             John Kessel (R)(DS*)
   (dischgd.7 Aug.)           Ferdinand Lepper **
John Andresor (R)(DS*)        Charles H. Martin (R)(DS*)
Edson F. Archer (R)#          Edmond McMath (R)(DS*)
Charles Banks                 Alexander McPeak
James D. Benson (R)(DS*)      Lansing A. Moore
Nathan J. Brown               Michael Murray (R)(DS*)
John Burkman                  James O'Neill (R)(DS*)
Michael M. Clancy (R)(DS*)#   Danny Putnam (R)(DS*)
Francis Dayton (R)#           George Ross (R)#
Frank E. Dow (R)(DS:Adj.HQ)      (Joined 30 June)
William Etzler                Robert Shultz (R)(DS*)#
Mills Franklin (R)(DS*)       Remly Sidelinger (R)(DS*)
Edwin Goyer (R)(DS*)          Henry Stoffel
Charles Gunther (R)(DS*)      Fred H. Tobey (R)(DS*)
Silas Hart (R)                Frank Tilton (R)(DS*)
Robert Johnson (R)(DS*)#      Hugh J. Watson (R)(DS*)#
James M. Jones (R)(DS*)       John Weidman (R)(DS*)#
Samuel S. Kaapp (R)(DS*)#     Edgar Wesince (R)
              Joel R. Whitcomb (R)#


(R) Recruits joined Column 2 August, unless marked with #, which
    indicates an earlier enlistment date of 30 June.
(DS*) Due to a lack of horses, the unmounted recruits were assigned
    guard duty on the steamboats, and/or 'Fort Beans'.
** DS at Powder River 'Camp Supply' hospital; rejoined Company after
    Battle of Little Big Horn.

## SEVENTH CAVALRY : COMPANY M

CAPT. THOMAS HENRY FRENCH (Comd'g)
1ST LT. EDWARD GUSTAVE MATHEY (Temp.Comd'g Co.C)

1st Sgt. John Ryan

| | |
|---|---|
| Sgt. John McGlone | Sgt. William Capes |
| Cpl. William Lalor | (from Yellowstone Supply |
| Trp. Charles Fischer | Depot, 30 July) |
| Trp. Henry C. Weaver | Sad. John Donahue |
| Cpl. Harrison Davis (appt. 1 August) | Cpl. Frank Neely |
| Cpl. Hugh N. Moore (appt. 6 August) | (appt. 1 August) |

### PRIVATES

| | |
|---|---|
| Joseph Bates | Robert Senn |
| Herman Binderald (R) | James Severs |
| Morris Cain | John Sivertson |
| Joseph Corley (R) | William Slaper |
| John Dolan (dischgd. 3 July) | Frank Sniffin |
| Jean B.D. Gallenne | Walter L. Sterland |
| Bernard Golden | Frank Stratton |
| George Heid | Levi Thornberry |
| Charles Kavannagh | Rollins L. Thorpe |
| Daniel Mahoney | George Weaver |
| Edward Pigford | James Weeks |
| William Robinson(Regt.HQ:hosp.) | John Whisten |
| Hobart Ryder(DS.Wagon Train:hosp.) | Ferdinand Widmayer |
| William W. Rye | Charles G. Wiedman |
| John Seamans | Charles Williams |

John Zametzer (Ill:Ft.Rice)

(R) Recruits joined Column 2 August.

(Deserters Apprehended)

James Miles, Private, apprehended 4 July, from Company G, Second
     Cavalry, under name of Pvt. Edward J. Hamilton.

TWENTY-SECOND INFANTRY : COMPANY E

CAPT. CHARLES J. DICKEY (Comd'g)

1st Sgt. George Lough

Sgt. Andrew Ryan                    Cpl. David McGrath
Sgt. Oswald Windfuhr                Cpl. Herbert Winfield
Sgt. Francis Mathews (dischgd 23 Aug.)   Cpl. James B. Dougherty
Sgt. Thomas Murphy                  Musc. Edwin F. Lang
              Musc. Antoine Prosper
              (ill on steamer 'Carroll')

PRIVATES

Francis Ainger (ill on 'Carroll')        Frederick Leber
John Barney                              Edward O'Brien
Charles Brady                            James O'Connell
George Briggs                            Patrick Owens
James Cahill                             William F. Skehan
William Clark                            John Smyth
Samuel Decator                           Charles W. Steward
William Dien                             Joseph Sturm
Aloah Flynn                              Patrick Tobin
Andrew J. Goodenough                     James Ward
Merritt E. Hinkley (ill on 'Carroll')    Adolf Weiler

(Discharged 3 Aug.)

Luther Cole (Pvt.)                         Julius Rall (Pvt.)
              Gustave Salzner (Pvt.)

TWENTY-SECOND INFANTRY : COMPANY F

CAPT. ARCHIBALD H. GOODLOE (Comd'g)
 (ill in field after 16 August)
2ND LT. EDWARD W. CASEY (Comd'g Co. since 23 Aug.)

Sgt. Philip Savelle (dischgd 14 Aug.)      Sgt. Patrick Kelly
Sgt. William Schott                        Cpl. Charles Morton
Sgt. Daniel Drewe                          Cpl. Richard M. Crawford
Sgt. Hiram Spangenberg                     Cpl. Earnest Durrslew
                    Cpl. John Matza

PRIVATES

Richard Bailey                     Frank Kelch
James Boyle                        Frederick Kopp
Thomas Buckles                     Samuel Lowden
Charles Bullock                    Martin Lyons (dischgd
Henry Burgo                            30 August)
Michael Cronin                     Charles Malin (ill,26 Aug.)
Patrick Donaghue                   Bernard McCann
James Douglas                      Martin McGowan
Timothy J. Dunn                    Jacob Mealy
Charles E. Graham                  Dennis O'Brien
William Gruel                      John Parle
Charles J. Hart                    Edward F. Reed
Jacob Huff                         Peter Steckham
William Hyner                      John Sullivan (dischgd
Charles W Jaeger                       23 August)
Thomas Keegan                      George W. Thiele
Adolf von Westernhagen             William H. Walsh

TWENTY-SECOND INFANTRY : COMPANY G


CAPT. CHARLES W. MINER (Comd'g)
1ST LT. BENJAMIN C. LOCKWOOD
2ND WILLIAM N. DYKMAN


Sgt. Isaac B. Henry (dischgd 23 Aug.)      Cpl. Thomas Couzens
Sgt. Ferdinand Hugler                      Cpl. Edward Carlin
Sgt. Robert Anderson                       Cpl. Jacques Gerster
Sgt. Willard E. Reed                       Cpl. James White
Sgt. James Ryder                           Musc. Louis Humfress
                    Musc. William Jamison


PRIVATES


James A. Adams                             Henrick Hanne
Henry Bainbridge                           John Kelly
John Baker                                 John J. Keith
Hugh Bates                                 George F. Kreasch
Henry Boucher                              Henry Lynch
Berthold Bury                              George Maybrook
Lewis Close                                John Merkling
Cornelius Collins                          Charles MacKinnon
John Donahue                               William O'Donnell
Martin Farrel                              James Shannon
Alvis Fisher                               William Smith
Anthony Gavin                              James E.A. Walker
Thomas Gould                               John Weidaw
David R. Hazeltine                         Edward M. Whipple
            James Scollin (dischgd. 23 Aug.)

TWENTY-SECOND INFANTRY : COMPANY H


CAPT. DEWITT C. POOLE (Comd'g)
1ST LT. OSKALOOSA M. SMITH


Sgt. Robert H. Allen            Sgt. Michael Hyland
Sgt. Herman Guetzey             Cpl. William J. Elgie
Sgt. Hugh McDonald              Cpl. John Maresh
Sgt. George Hathaway            Cpl. Joseph H. Geaged (sp)
                  Musc. Alfred Lapiene


PRIVATES


Frank Alcorn                    James Kirby
Peter Breen                     Gerhard Lammers
Charles Boss                    John Lempke
Edward Brereton                 Alexander Malcomson
John Belged                     Chrisoston Hunschey
Richard Dunn                    James McNulty
Samuel R. Drummond              Edward Nolan
Francis Dillon                  Patrick O'Connor
Charles Elwell                  John Robinson
William H. Grammer              Henry Rathman
Charles Hammer                  George Simmons
Samuel C. Hopkins               John Walton
Charles Just                    Hugh Smith (dischgd 23 Aug.

## TWENTY-SECOND INFANTRY : COMPANY I

CAPT. FRANCIS CLARKE (Comd'g)
1ST LT. WILLIAM CONWAY
2ND LT. JAMES C. MACKLIN *

1st Sgt. Richard H. McCougow

| | |
|---|---|
| Sgt. John LaMaire | Cpl. John O'Brien |
| Sgt. William McCauley | Cpl. Charles R. Munson |
| Sgt. Philip Lavella | Cpl. Emile Durand |
| Cpl. Julius Schon | Musc. Edward R. Smith |

### PRIVATES

| | |
|---|---|
| Louis Backer | Charles Klein |
| James Dixon | Wolfgang Mezs (sp) |
| Osborne C. Durning | John Maloney |
| James B. Emery | Patrick Murphy |
| Emil Felmacher | James I. O'Neill |
| Andrew Fitzpatrick | Gerrit Pliucker (sp) |
| Jonas Gearsley | William Reed |
| John A. Greene | John Sullivan |
| August Greuther (dischgd 27 Aug. near O'Fallon's Creek) | Abraham L. Van Horn |
| | Charles Valentine |
| Henry Harris | Charles W. Wieland |

Charles H. Worwood

* Court-martialed 6 August for "drunkeness on duty"--dismissed
  from the Service 20 November 1876; but restored in January 1877
  as 2nd lieutenant with Eleventh Infantry.

## TWENTY-SECOND INFANTRY : COMPANY K

CAPT. MOTT HOOTEN (Comd'g)
1ST LT. WILLIAM J. CAMPBELL
2ND LT. WILLIAM H. KELL


1st Sgt. William N. Davis

| | |
|---|---|
| Sgt. William Glenn | Cpl. John H. Smith |
| Sgt. Benjamin Herrins | Cpl. Frank Smith |
| Sgt. Robert Hannold | Musc. Charles Neerey |
| Cpl. Thomas Reid | Musc. Philip Petrie |


### PRIVATES

| | |
|---|---|
| William Acres | John Madden |
| John Bauer | Patrick Maley |
| Albert Berncisco | Patrick Malene |
| George Dachend | Miles Maloney |
| Edward Dark | John McCall |
| John Darney | John McGarrity |
| James Dorney | Bernard McManus |
| Patrick Dowden | Augustus Schucks |
| Michael Fitzimmens | John Schweitzer |
| Dennis Flanagan | Jeremiah Shields |
| James Kennedy | Sidney Smithson |
| Jacob Lewis | Albert Van Vert |
| Edward Malmiree | William Wilson |

## FIFTH INFANTRY : COMMAND

COL.(BVT.MAJ.GEN.) NELSON A. MILES  (Comd'g)

1ST LT. FRANK D. BALDWIN, Battalion Adjutant
CAPT. FORREST H. HATHAWAY, Quartermaster
2ND LT. THOMAS M, WOODRUFF, Engineering Officer

DR. LOUIS TESSON, Acting Surgeon

George M. Miles, Quartermaster Clerk


COMPANY B : CAPT. ANDREW S. BENNETT
            1ST LT. HENRY ROMEYN
            2ND LT. THOMAS M. WOODRUFF (Engr. Officer for HQ)

COMPANY E : 2ND LT. JAMES W. POPE

COMPANY F : CAPT. SIMON SNYDER
            1ST LT. EDWARD L. RANDALL
            2ND LT. FRANK S. HINKLE (joined 20 Aug.)

COMPANY G : CAPT. SAMUEL OVENSHINE
            1ST LT. THEODORE Y. FORBES

COMPANY H : 1ST LT. EDMUND RICE
            2ND LT. CHARLES E. HARGOUS

COMPANY K : 1ST LT. MASON CARTER
            2ND LT. JAMES A. WHITTEN (attached)

## FIFTH INFANTRY : COMPANY B

CAPT. ANDREW S. BENNETT (Comd'g)
1ST LT. HENRY ROMEYN
2ND LT. THOMAS M. WOODRUFF (Engr. Officer for HQ)

1st Sgt. James Scott

| | |
|---|---|
| Sgt. Charley McCoy | Cpl. Wernard Vogle |
| Sgt. Louis F. Ward | Cpl. Eugene C. Shiffer |
| Sgt. Henry Brown | Cpl. James Barrowman |
| Sgt. James Wilson | Musc. Edwin M. Brown (with HQ) |
| Cpl. George Kirkbride | Musc. John Potter |

### PRIVATES

| | |
|---|---|
| George Abel | Homer Lowell |
| John Anderson | Robert C. Malloy |
| George Bagley | John McCormick |
| John Bartley | Franklin J. McIntyre |
| Thomas J. Brading | John H. Miller |
| John Brophey | John M. Miller |
| James Bullen | John Mulligan |
| E.R. Capron | John S. Penwell |
| George C. Carty | Frederick A. Rieder |
| Stephen J. Coffey | Michael Ryan |
| Charles Collins | Charles Schmidt |
| Eli Covery | Joseph Schweigert |
| Amos Dinnsen | Herman Seegar |
| Thomas Doyale | Thomas Shea |
| Sumner B. Felt | Frederick Sieber |
| John Haddo | Arthur Ulitz |
| William Harris | Samuel J. Walter |
| Joseph Heinzmann | Isaac Weaver |
| John Hoalt | Charles Winter |
| Patrick Kelly | Manuel Young |

### (Attached to Co.B 2 August)

| | |
|---|---|
| John Cole | Frederick O. Hunt |
| James Conroy | Patrick Hegancy |
| Morris Dowd | William Knapp |
| Andrew J. Hinkle | Thomas Keegan |
| John Hughes | Charles Marsh |

Armour McFarland

## FIFTH INFANTRY : COMPANY E

### 2ND LT. JAMES W. POPE (Comd'g)

1st Sgt. Henry C. Thompson

| | |
|---|---|
| Sgt. Robert W. Phelan | Cpl. William F. Shipp |
| Sgt. Michael Farrell | Cpl. George H. Cohen |
| Sgt. John Sullivan | Cpl. Louis Amart |
| Sgt. Frank J. Steiger | Musc. Noah Liechty |

Musc. Thomas O. Saffell

### PRIVATES

| | |
|---|---|
| Mathias Ahab | Jacob Fullmer |
| Rudolph Amart | Thomas Griffin |
| John Andrews | John Harlin |
| Robert Bechinor | John Heinbaugh |
| Richard Bellows | Charles M. Henning |
| Frank Bigman | Leopold Hohman |
| Fred Bolling | James Hughes |
| James Brady | Mathew Kelly |
| William Brady | Edward McIntyre |
| James Butler | Michael McLaughlin |
| Edward Carpenter | Reuben J.D. Mitchell |
| John Q. Dempsey | James Murray |
| Stephen Donnelly | George Powers |
| Edward Dwyer | Patrick H. Ryan |
| John F. Fitzsimons | Edward H. Sands |
| George J. Ford | Isaac Staley |
| John Fraser | Charles J. Vickers |
| Alvah C. Frink | John Warren |

### (Attached from Co.H)

| | |
|---|---|
| John Ahern | John Ladd |
| Francis H. Farrington | John O'Neill |
| John Hogan | Timothy H. Pratt |
| Peter Johnson | Miles A. Radcliff |
| Patrick Keating | George E. White |

### (Attached from Co.C)

| | |
|---|---|
| Frank Fisher | William Reilly |

FIFTH INFANTRY : COMPANY F


CAPT. SIMON SNYDER (Comd'g)
1ST LT. EDWARD L. RANDALL
2ND LT. FRANK S. HINKLE (joined 20 Aug.)*


1st Sgt. John Unger

Sgt. John Brannigan               Cpl. Emil Roehm
Sgt. Joseph Stafford              Cpl. James Genand
Sgt. Jacob Vollinger              Cpl. Louis Pregler
Sgt. John D. Brooking             Musc. Adam A. Anderson
Cpl. John R. Reeves               Musc. Joseph Schopp


PRIVATES


Frank Austin                      Thomas J. Mains
William Baird                     Charles McIntee
Frederick Beck                    James C. Miller
Louis Borie                       James Moore
Hans Carsten                      Solomon Mosier
Richard Cogan                     William H. Mott
William G. Dustin                 Charles Olstad
Bartholemew Flynn                 Francis Payne
Patrick Fox                       Ernest Pier
Michael Giltman                   James A. Pope
James Gorman                      Edward Reeves
Adam Habergarten                  Aquilla Roberts
Michael Hamilton                  Joseph Ryan
John Harmon                       Joseph Schmidt
Jacob C. Hupman                   Ernest Siglock
Thomas Hurley                     Charles Smith
Frederick Jephson                 John B. Tepe
Joseph W. Levett                  Albert S. Wing
          Morris Wallen (ill on 'Carroll' 24 Aug.)


(Attached to Co.F)

John Mitchell (Sgt. Co.I)         Charles S. Gibbs (Pvt.Co.C
William H. Booth (Pvt. Co.E)      Michael Marlin (Pvt. Co.C)
Thomas Clark (Pvt. Co.C)          James O'Neill (Pvt.Co.C)
Francis Degner (Pvt. Co.C)        Frank Allen (Pvt.Co.C)
Gottlieb Holkins (Pvt. Co.C)      Albert Schardun (Pvt.Co.C)

* Departed Ft. Leavenworth 25 July, taken by steamer 'Carroll' as far
  as Glendive Creek, then, from 1st Lt. Edmund Rice's camp at 11 p.m.,
  rode all night with two Ree Indian scouts, and arriving at Terry's
  camp along the Powder River at 8 a.m. 20 August.

FIFTH INFANTRY : COMPANY G

CAPT. SAMUEL OVENSHINE (Comd'g)
1ST LT. THEODORE Y. FORBES

1st Sgt. Henry Hogan

Sgt. Denis Byrne                          Cpl. Alonzo Krause
Sgt. George Krager                        Cpl. Franz Engel
Sgt. Frank Tomlinson (DS,]3 Aug.)         Musc. Henry Weiss
                      Musc. Jesse O'Neil

PRIVATES

Charles Adams                             John S. McEwen
John Backer                               Walter H. Montgomery
Edward Bayer                              Lewis A. Noblette
Samuel W. Brenenstuhl                     Patrick Noonan
Richard Burke                             Edward O'Connor
Thomas J. Burke                           John O'Connor
Richard Callaghan                         Michael O'Donnell
James Cassidy                             Thomas O'Shaughnessy
Frank Commoch                             James Pennington
Thomas Cushing                            Richard W. Peshall
Sam Denny                                 James Quigley
John S. Donnelly                          Richard Quiena
James Dugan                               John F. Richon
Frank Gundera                             David Ryan
Albert Hansel                             Edward Schindler
Dan Horgan                                Michael Schuster
James Johnson                             David Spitser
Patrick Kane                              Franklin Tyler
John Malarkey                             Barney Wegman
William McAtee                            Joseph White
Michael McCormack                         Charles Zandt
        Dennis Shields (killed by Indian gunfire while
            escort guard 23 August on steamer 'Yellowstone')

(Attached to Co.G)

John Daly                                 George W. Stevens
Wilber H. Battey                          George Labegan
Oscar Bauer                               Ernest Schmidt
James Beatty (Pvt. Co.D)                  Anthony O'Malley (Pvt.Co.D)
George A. Bowers (Pvt. Co.D)              James Richards (Pvt.Co.D)
Michael Murray (Pvt. Co.D)                  (on steamer 'E.H.Durfee')

FIFTH INFANTRY : COMPANY H


1ST LT. EDMUND RICE (Comd'g)
2ND LT. CHARLES E. HARGOUS


1st Sgt. Charles J. Hatcher

| | |
|---|---|
| Sgt. Thomas Kelly | Cpl. Patrick Dunnigan |
| Sgt. William Hoyt | Cpl. Charles Wilson |
| Sgt. Adolph Marks | Cpl. Gerard K. Field |
| Cpl. William F. Knaur | Musc. William Edeler |

Musc. Charles Latham


PRIVATES


| | |
|---|---|
| Christian Bauer | Dennis Leary |
| Irwin L. Boyer | Henry T. Loomis |
| Henry Brooks | Michael Loftus |
| William J. Brooks | John Maker |
| James H. Burns | George Martin |
| Roddy Cox | Michael McNamara |
| Thomas F. Collins | Christopher McEvoy |
| Frank L. Comstock | Daniel McGinnis |
| George H. Dakna | Paul McShane |
| Thomas Dennis | John McTiernan |
| James M. Eddy | George Miller |
| John G. Egan | Daniel Moore |
| William Edwards | John J. Murphy |
| George Granger | Nathan B. Phillips (DS) |
| John Hanlin | John M. Roth |
| Albert Hickey | John Sheehan |
| Charles A. Hunt | John Frank |
| Alois Hug | George Walter |
| Enoch A. Joslin | Perry West |
| John Kearns | George W. Wilson |


(Attached to Co.H)


| | |
|---|---|
| Harvey Barnett | Charles M. Montrose |
| Joseph Brogan | Charles O. Dowd |
| Edward Hunt | Nicholas B. Wadr |


(Discharged)


| | |
|---|---|
| Henry Ameling (Pvt.) | Michael Herlihy (Pvt.) |

## FIFTH INFANTRY : COMPANY K

1ST LT. MASON CARTER  (Comd'g)
2ND LT. JAMES A. WHITTEN (attached) *

1st Sgt. Julius Barteman

| | |
|---|---|
| Sgt. Augustus Blohm | Cpl. George Wentzel |
| Sgt. Charles Arthur | Cpl. Levi H. Mease |
| Sgt. John Keeks | Cpl. Robert Walsh |
| Sgt. James B. Diebert | Musc. John King |
| Cpl. Eugene Allen | Musc. John Dishner |

### PRIVATES

| | |
|---|---|
| George H. Beble | William T. Mason |
| William Baster | Arthur Maynard |
| Frederick Backman | Henry Moore |
| Henry Boyd | Daniel Murphy |
| William H. Brown | James O'Sullivan |
| William H. Burgess | John Owens |
| Louis Busch | James Powers |
| Patrick Daily | William Riordan |
| James M. Dinsmore | Herman Stieffel |
| Martin Dorsey | Charles Semmber |
| Benjamin Duchman | Ralph Teeple |
| Paul Edwards | Alexander Tevaddeli |
| Joseph Gibson | Robert Wallace |
| John M. Hutchison | John Ward |
| Charles Hod | William H. Watson |
| Louis Holley | William F. Weed |
| James Jolly | Frederick Weise |
| John Krentz | Charles Wells |
| John Morah | Peter Wells |
| Andrew Hike | Leonard B. Whitback |

### (Attached to Co.K)

| | |
|---|---|
| Robert Wenderson | George Hamilton |
| Thomas Law[s] (Co.I) | Martin O'Brien |
| Cornelius Casey (ill on 'E.H.Durfee' | John Reynolds |
|    since 25 July) | Thomas Riley |
| John Covert | Edward Rooney |
| William H. Daily | John Hunselkuse |
| August C. Daniel | William J. Kane |

Hugh B. Ward

* Court-martialed for "drunkeness" 7 August. Resigned from the
  Service 31 May 1877.

## HEADQUARTERS COMMAND

BRIG.GEN. GEORGE CROOK (Comd'g)
1ST LT. JOHN GREGORY BOURKE (co.L, 3rd Cav.), Assist. Adj. General
2ND LT. WALTER SCRIBNER SCHUYLER (Co.B, 5th Cav.), Aide-de-Camp &
    5th Cavalry Liaison Officer
1ST LT. JOHN WILSON BUBB (Co.I, 4th Inf.), Act'g Commissary of
    Subsistence
CAPT. GEORGE MORTON RANDALL (Co.I, 23rd Inf.), Chief of Scouts and
    Shoshonee and Ute Indian Allies
MAJOR THADDEUS HARLAN STANTON (Paymaster, U.S.Army), Comd'g "irregular
    forces, composed of citizens, volunteers, and such others as may
    be assigned to him by Expedition Comdr."
MAJOR JOHN V. FUREY, Act'g Quartermaster and Ordnance Officer at the
    'Camp Cloud Peak' base camp

DR. BENNETT AUGUSTINE CLEMENTS, Medical Dir. for Expedition
DR.(MAJOR) ALBERT HARTSUFF, Assistant Surgeon
DR.(CAPT.) JULIUS HERMAN PATZKI, Assistant Surgeon
DR. CHARLES R. STEPHENS, Act'g Assist. Surgeon
DR. VALENTINE T. McGILLYCUDDY, Act'g Assist. Surgeon
DR. JUNIUS LEVERT POWELL, Act'g Assist. Surgeon
DR. R.B. GRIMES, Act'g Assist. Surgeon at 'Camp Cloud Peak'
DR. WILLIAM COOPER LECOMPTE, Act'g Assist. Surgeon ('Camp Cloud Peak')

THOMAS MOORE, Pack Train Master
CHARLES RUSSELL, Wagon Train Master ('Camp Cloud Peak')

## SCOUTS

William F.(Buffalo Bill) Cody        Louis Richaud ]Richard]
    (Chief Scout)                    Jonathan (Buffalo Chips) White
Frank Grouard                        'Capt. Jack' Crawford
Baptiste 'Big Bat' Pourier               (joined Column 9 August)
Baptiste 'Little Bat' Garnier        Chief Washakie (Shoshonee)
Tom Cosgrove (ex-Confederate Captain from Texas, with Shoshonee)
Louissant (Shoshonee)                Ben Arnold (courier)
Ed Seminole (courier)                _____ Fairbanks (courier)
'Capt.' Graves (miner)               _____ Young (packer)
'Shep' Medera (packer)

## CORRESPONDENTS

Joseph Wasson [Philadelphia Press; New York Tribune; San Francisco
        Alta California]
Cuthbert C. Mills[New York Times]  John F. Finerty [Chicago Times]
Barbour Lathrop [San Francisco Call-Bulletin]
J.J. Talbot [New York Graphic]
Reuben Davenport [New York Herald]
Robert E.'Alter Ego' Strahorn [Chicago Tribune; Denver Rocky Mountain
        News; New York Times; Cheyenne Sun

## FIFTH CAVALRY : REGIMENT ROSTER


COL.(BVT. MAJOR GEN.) WESLEY MERRITT (Comd'g)
LT.COL.(BVT. MAJOR GEN.) EUGENE ASA CARR (2nd in Comd.)

1ST LT. CHARLES KING (Co.K), Regimental Adjutant
1ST LT. WILLIAM CURTIS FORBUSH (Co.K), A.A.A.G.
1ST LT. WILLIAM PREBLE HALL (Co.E), Quartermaster
2ND LT. JULIUS HAYDEN PARDEE (23rd Inf.), A.D.C. to Gen. Merritt
2ND LT. ROBERT HUNTER YOUNG (4th Inf.), A.D.C. to Gen. Merritt

MAJOR JOHN V. UPHAM, Comd'g First Battalion
2ND LT. HOEL SMITH BISHOP (Co.G), Adjutant, First Battalion

MAJOR JULIUS WILMOT MASON, Comd'g Second Battalion
2ND LT. CHARLES DYER PARKHURST (Co.E), Adjutant, Second Battalion


### FIRST BATTALION

COMPANY A : CAPT. CALBRAITH PERRY RODGERS
            2ND LT. GEORGE O. EATON
COMPANY C : CAPT. EMIL ADAM
            2ND LT. EDWARD LIVINGSTON KEYES
COMPANY G : CAPT. EDWARD MORTIMER HAYES
COMPANY I : CAPT. SANFORD COBB KELLOGG
            1ST  LT. BERNARD REILLY, JR.(with Co.M since August)
            2ND  LT. ROBERT LONDON (with Co.D since 20 August)
            2ND  LT. SATTERLEE CLARK PLUMMER (4th Inf.),Attached
COMPANY M : CAPT. EDWARD HENRY LEIB


### SECOND BATTALION

COMPANY B : CAPT. ROBERT HUGH MONTGOMERY
            1ST LT. WILLIAM J. VOLKMAR
COMPANY D : CAPT. SAMUEL STORROW SUMNER
COMPANY E : CAPT. GEORGE FREDERIC PRICE
COMPANY F : CAPT. JOHN SCOTT PAYNE
            1ST LT. ALFRED BOYCE BACHE
COMPANY K : CAPT. ALBERT EMMETT WOODSON


### (SUPPORTING STAFF)

1ST LT. CHARLES H. ROCKWELL, Quartermaster Dept.
LIEUT. WILLIAM C. HUNTER (USN), Attached to Co.A

Sgt.Major Paul F.A. Humme
Quartermaster Sgt. John F.C.Rohrs
Sgt.Major Charles M. Smith, Veterinary Surgeon
Saddler Sgt. Jacob F. Rapp
Chief Trumpeter John Banse
Chief Musician Frederick W. Lewis

FIFTH CAVALRY : COMPANY A


CAPT. CALBRAITH P. RODGERS (Comd'g) *
2ND LT. GEORGE O. EATON **
LIEUT. WILLIAM C. HUNTER (USN), Attached


1st Sgt. Thomas Murnane

| | |
|---|---|
| Sgt. John F. Smith | Cpl. Henry Seekange |
| Sgt. John Powers | Cpl. Samuel M. Spencer |
| Sgt. John Connolly | Cpl. Oscar von Melbach |
| Sgt. John Moore | Trp. John Johnson |
| Sgt. Edward Thompson | Sad. Frederick Schmid |

Blksm. John Weber


PRIVATES


| | |
|---|---|
| John W. Adams | Gustave Koekler |
| Patrick Adams | Francis Loving |
| Charles N. Aller | James F. Lumior |
| Michael Bryan | Christian Madsen |
| William H. Chaffin | John Maher |
| Henry Chappel | Samuel W. Mason |
| John Clark | Patrick McCoran |
| Charles T. Coble | Michael McGrail |
| William H. Collins | Joseph McKnight |
| William Cunningham | John McLure |
| Timothy Delaney | Cyrus Milink |
| James Donlay (HQ Mess) | James Morsell |
| John Donnelly | James Noonan |
| Henry Finnegan | James H. North |
| John Fitzgerald | Henry O'Neil |
| Conrad Fortson | John D. Parrum |
| Jacob Fritz | James Patterson |
| Lewis Fritz | Thomas Riley |
| William Hasting | William T. Rollins |
| Thomas Hearn | John Ryan |
| John Keith | Francis M. St.Clair |
| John Kenecht | Martin Schmidt |

Julius Schweiker


* Robert R. Wilson, Captain, resigned 1 July, to take effect 29 July.
** Disabled on night of 10 August, when horses stampeded from camp.
   During the excitement, Eaton's revolver discharged, tearing off a
   portion from the right hand's index finger. He left the Column on
   24 August on the steamer 'Carroll' with the other disabled.

FIFTH CAVALRY : COMPANY B


CAPT. ROBERT HUGH MONTGOMERY (Comd'g)
1ST LT. WILLIAM J. VOLKMAR (DS)


1st Sgt. John McConnell

| | |
|---|---|
| Sgt. Jacob Marbock | Cpl. Francis H. DeCaskey |
| Sgt. Theodore Schedwick | Cpl. Joseph S. Clanton |
| Sgt. Julius B. Weil | Cpl. Jerome Lawler |
| Sgt. Henry P. Butler * | Trp. Jacob Busch |
| Sgt. James Ainley | Far. Albert Jarvis |
| Cpl. James Sloan | Far. George Jarvis |

Sad. John Branshoop


PRIVATES


| | |
|---|---|
| Cornelius Ames | Frederick H. Lynch |
| John Armsbury | Martin Malaw |
| John Bakovsky | Martin Malentovic |
| Ernest H. Chapman | James Martinak |
| John Dahl | John McDonald * |
| Richard Dallam | Henry McElroy |
| Robert V. Elliott | Andrew J. Merritt |
| George Emory | Joseph W. Miller |
| William W. Eraus | Patrick Murphy |
| Thomas Flemming | Claude M. Pettibone |
| James Fox * | Albert Ruckesback |
| William Fry | Edward Schmidt |
| Maught Haakinson | Christopher Sheppard |
| John Hall | Robert Olson Snyder |
| George W. Kales | James Stavnois |
| William B. Kempe | James Stephanic |
| Richard Killiganey | Charles Thealman |
| Charles C. Knowles | James Thompson |
| Martin Koch | Byron Tud |
| Nichan Laguer | Horace Tyler |
| Henry A. Lamandon | Edward Wordy |


* Received "Honorable Mention" for action on the mesa, 20 August 1874, near new road from Camp Verde to Camp Apache, Ariz. Terr.

## FIFTH CAVALRY : COMPANY C

CAPT. EMIL ADAM (Comd'g) (joined Regt.7 July)
2ND LT. EDWARD LIVINGSTON KEYES
(temporary comd. until 7 July)

1st Sgt. Francis Fox

| | |
|---|---|
| Sgt. Frank Bayles | Cpl. Robert Tobin |
| Sgt. Frederick Post | Cpl. Dennis B. Lorden |
| Sgt. Arthur Benton | Trp. John Futterer |
| Sgt. Heinrich Schenberg | Trp. Frederick Louis * |
| Sgt. Francis Flatley | Far. Edward White |
| Cpl. Frank C. Burdick | Blksm. William Netherly |
| Cpl. John Welch | Sad. Lewis M. Barre |

Wag. John Lee

### PRIVATES

| | |
|---|---|
| Henry Anderson | Edward Kennedy |
| Lewis C. Boone * | John Leary |
| William C. Bounsall | William S. Leonard ** |
| Cornelius Bernett | George F. Lowee |
| Alfred W. Carpenter | Henry Meyering |
| Michael Carroll | Otto Milwert |
| James C. Cary * | Wilhelm Neibuhr |
| John Catarious | Henry Nelson * |
| Ellis Cole | Albert Nunke |
| Richard L. Davis (ill, 24 Aug.) | John Ott * |
| John F. Donnelly | Henry Procter * |
| Joseph Foley | George Regien (DS Regt.HQ) |
| James Glynn | James P. Roberts |
| Edwin A. Green | Ross H. Roof |
| James Griffith | August Schneider * |
| Charles Haddock | William L. Scottin |
| Emerson G. Harper | Hans Simmonson *** |
| Joseph B. Hedley | John Smith * |
| Charles Hicks * | William Smith |
| George C. Howard * | Frederick Sutcliffe * |
| Christian Johnson | George Williams |
| George Keith | George Woods |

John Woods

\* Rejoined Regiment 28 July from DS
\*\* Ill at Goose Creek. Wounded in left leg below knee by accidental
   discharge of carbine while on guard ] August near Clear Creek,W.T.
\*\*\* Sick since 28 August. Sent to gov't asylum, Washington,D.C.

FIFTH CAVALRY : COMPANY D


CAPT. SAMUEL STORROW SUMNER (Comd'g)
2ND LT. ROBERT LONDON (temp. assignment since 20 June)


1st Sgt. Jacob Widmer

| | |
|---|---|
| Sgt. John Devine | Cpl. Charles Constantine |
| Sgt. James W. Wheeler | Cpl. John J. Lawton |
| Sgt. John Hamilton | Cpl. John P. Kelly |
| Sgt. Eurose F. Yeoman | Trp. Galen R. Wiseman |
| Sgt. John Morgan | Blksm. Victor Monteith |
| Cpl. Lindset W.C. Beckham | Far. Edward Martin |

Sad. James B. Frew


PRIVATES


| | |
|---|---|
| Christian Ahrens | Samuel Hood |
| Ernest Arold | James Jeffers |
| Franz Backer | Daniel Lane |
| James M. Bamford | Francis Levalley |
| Jacob Barmetter | Thomas Lynch |
| Frederick Bernhardt | John Lyons |
| Samuel Bradeen | Thomas McCabe |
| William H. Breed | Thomas Mooney |
| John Carroll | Ernest Muller |
| George Cloutier | Thomas Murphy |
| William Dalton | Joseph B. Patrick |
| Thomas J. Doughty | George W.A. Peck |
| Rudolph Eberhardt | John Remy |
| John Fagan | James H. Richardson |
| William Folckman | Peter D. Shields |
| Alexander Fulton | George Snider |
| Francis Garvey | James Ten Eyck |
| James G. Gibbs | Samuel P. Thomson |
| Edward Gilman | Gamaliel Tracy |
| Charles M. Gilbert | George White |
| William H. Glenn | George C. Wilday |
| John H. Harris | Thomas Williams |
| Henry Harrison | John H. Wilton |
| Joseph Harrison | Dennis Laffan (reduced from Cpl. 3 July) |

(Deserted from Ft. Fetterman 28 July)

Charles E. Baccehh (Pvt.)              Charles Gerhardt (Pvt.)
Alexander Harker (Pvt.)

FIFTH CAVALRY : COMPANY E

CAPT. GEORGE FREDERIC PRICE (Comd'g)
2ND LT. CHARLES DYER PARKHURST (Adjutant, 2nd Battalion)

1st Sgt. Frank E. Hill

| | |
|---|---|
| Sgt. Charles Miller | Cpl. George M. Smith |
| Sgt. William H. Potts | Cpl. William L. Day |
| Sgt. John Francis | Trp. Albert D. Fosbenner |
| Sgt. Charles H. Gardner | Trp. Emil Schimpoff |
| Sgt. Thomas Quinn | Sad. Thomas Ghortill |
| Cpl. John C. Pope | Far. James Woller |
| Cpl. George W. Beckman | Blksm. Edward Gafferly |

PRIVATES

| | |
|---|---|
| Benjamin F. Bird | Earnest Hattier |
| Thomas Brady | George Hearst |
| Anton Brown | Robert W. Heath |
| Richard Buckminster | George A. Hunter |
| James Carney | Henry W. Jefferson |
| William C. Casey | Miles W. Jenkins |
| William H. Clark | Frederick Kade |
| Edward Coffan | Edward L. McLaughlin |
| David Condon | Alfred McMackin |
| Marcus Culpepper | Frederick F. Mier |
| James P. Dean | William Miles |
| Abraham Duffour | Joseph Murray |
| Michael Duffy | Walter A. North |
| Theodore Drager | James O'Neill |
| John Feighery | William Pickens |
| Isaac H. Fenton | Simon C. Ruffner |
| Oliver Fillman | Joseph Schlacker |
| Oliver G. Flemming | John Shay |
| Maurice Foley | Edward Stanton |
| Thomas Grant | Daniel Stewart |
| John Guinnin | William H. Winters |
| John Harris | Patrick Young |

(Deserted at Cheyenne, W.T.)

William F. Hickman (Pvt.)

FIFTH CAVALRY : COMPANY F


CAPT. JOHN SCOTT PAYNE (Comd'g)
1ST LT. ALFRED BOYCE BACHE


1st Sgt. Joseph Bradley *+

| | |
|---|---|
| Sgt. Andrew P. Duggan | Cpl. Simpson Hornaday |
| Sgt. George Yearsley | Cpl. Charles J. Seuter (sp) |
| Sgt. Michael Sluiky (sp) | Trp. Theodore Kash |
| Sgt. William S. Taylor | Trp. Michael Donnelly |
| Sgt. Ford Hampford | Far. Hamilton B. Murphy |
| Cpl. John Merrill | Blksm. Philip Kerwin |

Sad. Michael Dougherty


PRIVATES


| | |
|---|---|
| Thomas Barrett + | Henry Lowell |
| John Butler | John S. Marshall |
| Frank Cainwell | Neil Matheson ** |
| James Collins | John McGrady |
| Albert Czaia | George Miller |
| Matthew Daily | Patrick Moriarity |
| William H. Day | John Murray |
| John Duffy | Thomas Murray |
| Franklin Fergusson ** | John Nihill |
| Daniel Ford | Amos Nunemaker |
| Henry Fulk | Francis A. Odell |
| Henry E. Fuller | Walter Peterson |
| Michael T. Gilligan | John A. Poppe |
| John Harrington | Hampton A. Roach |
| Samuel Hay | William Roberts |
| John Hoady | William F. Rogers |
| Charles Johnson | George William Russell |
| Samuel Klingensmith | John Smith |
| Mathew Kreiger | Peter Smith |
| Emil Kussman | David Stephens |
| David Links (sp) | John Texton |
| Robert Longstaff | Robert H. Walker |

Hugh Weir


* Marked gallantry, Apache Creek, A.T., 2 April 1874
+ Sycamore Springs, Mazatzal Mtns, A.T., 20 October 1873. Commended
  for good conduct. Bradley was a Private then.
** Ill at Yellowstone Camp on Powder 23 August

FIFTH CAVALRY : COMPANY G


CAPT. EDWARD MORTIMER HAYES (Comd'g)
2ND LT. HOEL SMITH BISHOP (Adjutant, First Battalion)


1st Sgt. Charles Miller

Sgt. Timothy Casey                    Cpl. Henry H. Hale
Sgt. Charles Abbott                   Cpl. William Langton
Sgt. John C. Kelson                   Trp. Samuel Myers
Sgt. James Rodgers                    Far. Albert J. Henry
Cpl. John Cridland                    Wag. Charles Whiting


PRIVATES


Thomas Baker                          John R. Higbee
Albert E. Barker                      John Higgson
Charles Bidwell                       John R. Jones
Philander Bidwell                     Henry Kaufman
Edward Boland                         James Keefe
Edward Bond                           Samuel B. Lamprey
William Brass                         Joseph Mayer
Thomas Brodrick                       Edward C. McDonald
Daniel Brown (DS Regt.HQ)             Thomas McFarlin
Frank J. Brown                        John McGilligan
John Collins                          Edward McNulty
William H. Crimp                      James Morrow
Richard Cunningham (DS Regt.HQ)       Eugene Moulton
James E. Derwent *                    John Myers
Thomas Doherty                        Edward Newman
Henry B. East **                      Jeremiah O'Brien
Anthony Fennel                        John O'Connor
Phillip A. Flood                      John Sharron
George Frazier                        Jacob Stakley
Thomas Halvey                         James Stewart
John Hiet                             John A. Weaver
                    Benjamin F. Tierson


* Reduced from Sgt.Major (Fort Hays, Kans.) 16 May 1876
** Reduced from Cpl. (Fort Hays, Kans.) 26 May 1876

## FIFTH CAVALRY : COMPANY I

CAPT. SANFORD COBB KELLOGG (Comd'g)
1ST LT. BERNARD REILLY, JR. (With Co.M since August)
2ND ROBERT LONDON (With Co.D since 20 June)
2ND LT. SATTERLEE CLARK PLUMMER (Co.A, 4th Inf.)
     (Attached)


1st Sgt. Daniel F. Shine

Sgt. Maurice L. Pivone *             Cpl. Joseph Shaddock
Sgt. John Graham                    Cpl. Samuel Fellhart
Sgt. Henry Bremer                   Sad. Henry Marcer
Sgt. Robert A. Carnahan             Blksm. Carl Leille
Sgt. Charles Roisvetter             Far. E.G. White (en route)
Cpl. Oliver H. Bwaver (sp)          Trp. Alfred Milner
Cpl. Jakob Blaut                    Trp. Patrick Bradley


### PRIVATES

Harvey Adams                        Barney Korslager
Aion (sp) Alex                      Christian A. Larson
John A. Artmoin                     Patrick Maley
Frank Barringer **                  Ellis McCurdy
Herman Bauman                       Donald McDonald
Mathew Blake                        Eland (sp) McNamee
Frederick Bower                     Charles Meckel
Charles Bunger                      Haymes (sp) Nordegeski
Andrew Carroll                      John Pommer
Charles Conahan                     Robert H. Priest
William Douglas                     John M. Roberts
John Dusold                         Charles V. Robinson
Daniel Fillery                      James Stark
John Haley                          John W. Strait
James Harvey                        Charles Stuart
John Hoffman                        Joseph Sullivan
Neil C. Jensen                      Ben A. Wanamaker
Harvey King                         William Wessell
                William J. Watts


\* Reduced from 1st Sgt. 15 May 1876
\*\* Joined Regt. near Fort Fetterman 14 July

FIFTH CAVALRY : COMPANY K

CAPT. ALBERT EMMETT WOODSON (Comd'g) ***

1st Sgt. Rudolph Stauffer *

| | |
|---|---|
| Sgt. Edmund Schreiber ** | Cpl. Thomas W. Wilkinson |
| Sgt. James Kelly | Cpl. Patrick Hickia |
| Sgt. Leon W. Wierson | Cpl. James Lenihan |
| Sgt. Daniel McGrath | Sad. James Sands |
| Sgt. John F. Kogan | Blksm. Osker C. Hart |
| Cpl. Thomas McCormick | Far. Edward McGuire |

Trp. August Rauden

PRIVATES

| | |
|---|---|
| William Aischiff | Arthur McMahon |
| Jacob Auberg | James McQade |
| Simon Calnon | Michael McQuay |
| James Caniff | Henry Meraker |
| Joseph Coyle | John D. Murphy |
| John Cryden | Adano Palle |
| Thomas Daly | John Press |
| John Darcey | Patrick Reilly |
| Patrick Dooley | Thomas Salmon |
| James Duffy | Mathias Schmitz |
| Joseph Eubin (sp) | Malcolm Smith |
| George L. Granberry | Jacob Stendla |
| George Greancy | Jeremiah Sullivan |
| John Grey | August E. Tetner |
| George Heinemann | John Wallace |
| Henry Imsauda | Leon Waitsour |
| John H. Juergeus (sp) | William Ward |
| Patrick Maua | Henry O. Webb |
| Taylor Mautler | Peter Weekoft |
| Dennis Minnihaw | Peter H. Wray |
| John McDermott | Robert Wright |

* (1) Near Tonto Creek, 9 May 1874; (2) Summit of Stauffer's Butte,
  NW of Diamond Butte, 25 May 1874: "Led charge & was first man on
  summit." (3) Black Mesa, near east branch of Verde River, 3 June
  1874. Honorable Mention.
** Canyon Creek, A.T., 10 January 1874. Honorable Mention.
*** Capt. Julius Mason relinquished command of Co.K, per verbal
  instructions 5 August 1876 from HQ. Promoted Major, Fifth Cav.,
  to date from 1 July, and given command of Second Battalion.

## FIFTH CAVALRY : COMPANY M

CAPT. EDWARD HENRY LEIB (Comd'g)
2ND LT. CHARLES WATTS (ill at Ft. Lyons: pistol
    discharged & wounded him 7 July)
1ST LT. BERNARD REILLY, JR.(Attached since August)


1st Sgt. Thomas Considine

| | |
|---|---|
| Sgt. Albert Stark | Cpl. Charles Wilson |
| Sgt. Isaac B. Lewis | Cpl. Albert Chamberlain |
| Sgt. William M. Connolly | Sad. Christopher Edele |
| Sgt. Charles P. Huntington * | Blksm. John C. Houts |
| Sgt. William J. Sherry (appt. 1 Aug.) | Far. Frank Smith |
| Cpl. Thomas Maloney | Trp. Julius Erb |

Trp. Paul Schneider


### PRIVATES

| | |
|---|---|
| Thomas Allbring | John Healy |
| Sylvester Arnold | Edward Henry |
| Heinrich Backer · | Henry Hiners |
| Henry M. Bourke | Daniel Klein |
| Leopold Buttner | William Madden |
| Julius Cardinal | James H. McDonald |
| David Enos | James O'Neil |
| Joseph Fleming | Daniel Ort |
| Frederick G. Fussel | George W. Patterson |
| Francis Gallagher | Charles Quigley |
| Charles J. Gardiner | George Ressel |
| Winfield S. Gibbs | Joseph Reuter |
| James Gibson | Joseph Robinson |
| John Goldsmith ** | Frederick P. Sanders *** |
| Martin V. Greene | Frederick W. Shaw |
| Augustus S. Gunn | John Smith |
| Joseph E. Harrington | James Stewart |


* "...marked gallantry during action...", Apache Creek, A.T. 2 April
  1874
** Ill at Goose Creek camp, 5 August.
*** Reduced from Sgt. 7 July at Sage Creek

SECOND CAVALRY : BATTALION COMMAND


CAPT. HENRY ERASTUS NOYES (Co.I) (Comd'g)

COMPANY A : CAPT. THOMAS BULL DEWEES
            1ST LT. MARTIN EDWARD O'BRIEN
            2ND LT. DANIEL CROSBY PEARSON
COMPANY B : 1ST LT. WILLIAM CHARLES RAWOLLE
COMPANY C : 1ST LT. SAMUEL MILLER SWIGERT
            2ND LT. HENRY DUSTAN HUNTINGTON
COMPANY E : CAPT. ELIJAH REVILLO WELLS
            2ND LT. FREDERICK WILLIAM SIBLEY
COMPANY I : CAPT. HENRY ERASTUS NOYES (Comd'g Battalion)
            2ND FRED WILLIAM KINGSBURY


THIRD CAVALRY : BATTALION COMMAND


MAJOR ANDREW WALLACE EVANS (3rd Cav.) (Comd'g)
2ND LT. GEORGE FRANCIS CHASE (Co.L, 3rd Cav.),Adjutant

COMPANY A : 1ST LT. JOSEPH LAWSON
            2ND LT. CHARLES MORTON (QM & Aide-de-Camp to Col. Royall)
COMPANY B : CAPT. CHARLES MEINHOLD
            1ST LT. ALBERT DOUGLAS KING (Co.I)(Spec.Duty with Co.B)
COMPANY C : CAPT. FREDERICK VAN VLIET
COMPANY D : 2ND LT. JAMES FERDINAND SIMPSON
            2ND LT. WILLIAM WALLACE ROBINSON, JR.
COMPANT E : CAPT. ALEXANDER SUTORIUS (Court-matialed in field)
            1ST LT. ADOLPHUS H. VON LUETTWITZ (Co.C)(Comd'g )
COMPANY F : 1ST LT. ALEXANDER DALLAS BACHE
            2ND LT. BAINBRIDGE REYNOLDS
COMPANY G : 1ST LT. EMMET CRAWFORD
COMPANY I : CAPT. WILLIAM HOWARD ANDREWS
            2ND LT. JAMES EVANS HERON FOSTER
COMPANY L : CAPT. PETER DUMONT VROOM
COMPANY M : CAPT. ANSON MILLS
            1ST LT. AUGUSTUS CHOTEAU PAUL
            2ND LT. FREDERICK SCHWATKA


CAVALRY BRIGADE COMMAND


LT.COL. WILLIAM BEDFORD ROYALL (3rd Cav.)
2ND LT. HENRY ROWAN LEMLY (Co.E, 3rd Cav.), Adjutant
2ND LT. CHARLES MORTON (Co.A, 3rd Cav.), QM & Aide-de-Camp

## SECOND CAVALRY : COMPANY A

CAPT. THOMAS BULL DEWEES (Comd'g)
1ST LT. MARTIN EDWARD O'BRIEN
2ND LT. DANIEL CROSBY PEARSON


                    1st Sgt. Charles A. Maude (appt.19 July)

Sgt. Gregory P. Harrington                Cpl. Antonio Brogerri
  (resigned as 1st Sgt.19 July)           Cpl. Charles Angus
Sgt. William H. Butterworth               Cpl. John Naaf
Sgt. Alexander Albrecht                   Trp. John W. Vincent
Sgt. John A. Carr                         Trp. William F. Somers
Sgt. James Ellis                            (Ill 24 Aug.on'Far West')
Cpl. Charles Wintermute                   Blksm. Bernard Schnable
  (Ill 23 Aug.on'Far West')               Sad. Frederick France


### PRIVATES


Charles Austin                        Christopher McIntyre
James Branagan                        William H. Merritt
Henry C. Campbell                     Daniel Morgan
Marvin Collins                        Daniel Munger
John A. Courtney                      John Murphy
Thomas J. Dickinsen                   David W. Neil
Uriah Donaldson                       Robert Noonan
John Durkin (DS Wagon Train,Goose Cr.)  William F. Norwood
Henry Glock                           William J. Porter
Hugh Green                            William L. Regan
George Greenbauer (DS Wagon Train)    Michael Reynolds
James Hayes                             (DS Wagon Train)
James P. Henry (DS Wagon Train)       George B. Robinson
John Kelley                           Thomas A. Secord
Charles King                          Thomas Simpson (R)
Ferdinand Knupper                     Charles Spencer
Edward Lewis                          George W. Sweeney
Rudolph Laffelbein                    John F. Vincent
Thomas Lynch (R)                      Alonzo A. Vincent
Henry A. McCook (Commis.Dept.)        James Walsh
James McDuff                          John Wray


(R) Recruits who joined Column 3 August.

## SECOND CAVALRY : COMPANY B

### 1ST LT. WILLIAM CHARLES RAWOLLE (Comd'g)

1st Sgt. Bartholomew Shannon (appt. 22 July)

| | |
|---|---|
| Sgt. Alexander Huntington(appt.22 July) | Cpl. James Mitchell |
| Sgt. William J. Cunningham | Cpl. Eugene H. Glasure |
| Sgt. Charles W. Day | Trp. Robert Dyer |
| Sgt. Thomas Murray | Trp. John Friegel |
| Sgt. John Howard | Far. Charles F. Jones |
| Cpl. Thomas Aughey | Blksm. Edmund Grady |
| Cpl. William Cogan(appt.22 July) | Sad. John Grannickstadten |

### PRIVATES

| | |
|---|---|
| John Alten | Alexander Graham |
| Daniel Austin | Paul Gutike |
| Henry Baldwin | Francis Hart |
| Henry Chambers | Patrick Hasson |
| Henry G. Collins | Herman Herhold |
| James Conniff | William A. Hills |
| Charles P. Corliss | Thomas Kelly |
| James Cosgriff | Eggert Kohler |
| Robert Coster | Theodore P. Leighton |
| William Coulter | William H. Lyman |
| Louis Craft | Daniel McCleery |
| Richard H. Creswell | Henry Moos |
| John Davis | Francis O'Connor |
| Benjamin Domeck | James Ramer |
| Patrick Doherty | Peter J. Redmond |
| William F. Doughty | George W. Rowbee |
| Charles F. Edwards | Mark B. Rue |
| Adam Fox | William H. Tailor |
| Wesley Gable | Augustus Thompson |
| Thomas B. Glover | George D. Vickers |
| Michael Graemer | Patrick Wall |

Herbert Witmer

## SECOND CAVALRY : COMPANY D

1ST LT. SAMUEL MILLER SWIGERT (Comd'g)
2ND LT. HENRY DUSTAN HUNTINGTON

1st Sgt. James H. Carey

| | |
|---|---|
| Sgt. Frederick W. Evans | Cpl. William T. Webb |
| Sgt. John L. Joosteen | Cpl. James Galvin(appt.18July) |
| Sgt. George A. Williams | Trp. Gustavus Nicolai |
| Sgt. Rosell W. Payne | Trp. Joseph A. Wadsworth |
| Cpl. Henry E. Warrington | Sad. Henri Heynemann |
| Cpl. William Medigar | Far. William L. Webb |

Blksm. Charles E. Parker(appt.22 July)

### PRIVATES

| | |
|---|---|
| James Anthony | William Lang |
| William W. Burke (R) | Joseph Laverty |
| Otis W. Clarke | John Lewis |
| Michael Connors | Jacob Mack |
| Oscar R. Cornwell | Frank Mackenzie |
| (reduced from Sgt.18 July) | William Madden |
| Jeremiah Cory (Ill,Goose Creek) | John McCormack |
| Samuel J. Curtis | George McKnight |
| James Darcey | William McManus |
| George Daum | William A. Moffitt |
| Henry DeMott | John Moore |
| William Dudley | John C. Putnam |
| John Flemming | Emile Renner |
| James Forristel | John Shields |
| William Fryling | George A. Stone |
| Carl Hecht | Carlton Torman |
| Samuel W. Hone | Joseph Ward |
| Eugene Isaac | Edward A. Watson |
| John Jackson | Thomas H. White |
| Abraham Jacobs | William H. Williams |
| Washington Jones | James Wilson |
| Henry Kee | Joseph Wilson |
| James Keenan | John F.A. Witt |

(R) Recruit who joined Column 3 August.

## SECOND CAVALRY : COMPANY E

CAPT. ELIJAH REVILLO WELLS (Comd'g)
2ND LT. FREDERICK WILLIAM SIBLEY

1st Sgt. William Land

| | |
|---|---|
| Sgt. William P. Cooper | Cpl. William C. Kingsley |
| Sgt. George Howard | Cpl. Otto C. Mendhoff |
| Sgt. Weaver Dollmair | Cpl. Jacob Heird(appt. 1 Aug.) |
| Sgt. Orson M. Smith | Trp. Peter Waag |
| Sgt. John Hollenbecker(appt. 1 Aug.) | Sad. Joseph F. Long |

### PRIVATES

| | |
|---|---|
| Leo Baader | Montgomery McCormick (with HQ) |
| John Boch | Thomas McCue |
| Nicholas Burbach | William C. Murray |
| Patrick L. Clark | Edward Nagle |
| George Coyle | Richard Parrington |
| William I. Croley | William F. Paul |
| Lawrence Deloney | Linden B. Perry (with HQ) |
| William J Dougherty | Oliver Remley (R) |
| George E. Douglas | Cody Robertson |
| Milton F. Douglass | Oscar Rollan |
| William T. Englehorn | George Rosendale |
| Frank Forster | Valentine Rufus |
| Daniel Gabriel | Charles H. Sargent |
| Louis Gilbert(resigned Sgt.1 Aug.) | James A. Scott |
| John Glancey | James Smith * |
| David Hogg (hosp. duty) | Patrick Sullivan |
| John Hoffman | Charles Tausher |
| Howard Knapp | Jeremiah Twiggs |
| Alfred Logan | James Vance |
| Gustav Martini | William Volmer |

Hugo Wagner

(R) Recruit who joined Column 3 August.
* Joined Column 3 August from Cavalry Depot.

SECOND CAVALRY : COMPANY I


CAPT. HENRY ERASTUS NOYES (Comd'g Second Battalion)
2ND LT.FRED WILLIAM KINGSBURY (Comd'g Company)


1st Sgt. William Kirkwood

Sgt. Hugh McGrath                    Cpl. Amos Black
Sgt. William Taylor                  Cpl. Thomas C. Marrion
Sgt. George Cooper                   Cpl. John P. Slough
Sgt. William Skinner                 Far. George Fisher
Sgt. Thomas Meagher *                Sad. Henry Knapper


PRIVATES


Hermann Ashkey                   Charles Morrison
George M. Bickford               Gustav Ohm
Phillip Burnett                  James H. Ray
John E. Collins                  John Reynolds
Charles Emmons                   George Rhode
Frank W. Foss                    Gottlieb Ruf
John Gallagher                   John Russell
Charles G. Graham                Konrad Schmid
John G. Hall                     John M. Stevenson
Robert Johnson                   Irvine H. Stout
Walter B. Keenright              Patrick H. Wall
George H. Liddle                 Daniel Walsh
Martin Maher                     George J. Walters
Charles Minarcik                 George Watts
John Moran                       Thomas Wingfield


* Wounded 17 June (Battle of Rosebud).Hosp.Ft.Fetterman 27 June.

## THIRD CAVALRY : COMPANY A

1ST LT. JOSEPH LAWSON (Comd'g)
2ND LT. CHARLES MORTON
(Special duty as AAGM to 2nd & 3rd Cav. Battalions)


1st Sgt. John W. Van Moll

| | |
|---|---|
| Sgt. Henry Shafer | Cpl. Charles Bessey |
| Sgt. Gottlieb Bigalsky | Cpl. William H. Finch |
| Sgt. William J. Armstrong | Trp. Walter Wells |
| Sgt. Charles Anderson | Trp. George Hammer |
| Cpl. John Patton | Sad. Karl Dreher |

Blksm. Michael Conway


## PRIVATES

| | |
|---|---|
| James Allen | George D. Kaufman (R) |
| John Anderson | Lawrence Kennedy |
| William Babcock | Herman J. Kinder |
| Conrad Baker | Charles Kolaugh |
| Frederick Bartlett | Henry Leonard |
| John Bigley | John H. Louder |
| William A. Bills (R) | John Lynch * |
| Robert Blackwood(Ill,Goose Cr.) | John McCann |
| Joseph Boyle | Florence Neiderst |
| Maurice Breshnahan | Samuel Peterson * |
| John Cook | Henry Ramston (DS, Regt.Clk) |
| William Davis | John Reilly |
| John Downey | James L. Roberts |
| William Featherall | Albert Simons |
| Michael Fitzgerald | James E. Snepp |
| James Golden | Alfred S. Southon |
| Charles Gordon | James Taggart |
| Lawrence L. Grazierni | Ernest Therion ** |
| Edwin M. Griffin | William H. Vance |
| Thomas Gynan | John Wenzel |
| Maurice Hastings | George White |
| Robert Harry Hinze | James Wood |


(R) Recruits who joined Column 3 August.
* Ill, Yellowstone camp, 27 Aug.
** DS at Regt. Learning music.

THIRD CAVALRY : COMPANY B


CAPT. CHARLES MEINHOLD (Comd'g)
1ST LT. ALBERT DOUGLAS KING (Co.I) (Special Duty with
     Co.B since 4 August 1876)
2ND LT. JAMES FERDINAND SIMPSON (Comd'g Co.D)


1st Sgt. Charles Witzemann

| | |
|---|---|
| Sgt. John Moriarity | Cpl. Joseph Kirby |
| Sgt. Maurice Connell | Cpl. George G. Criswell |
| Sgt. James A. Boggs | Trp. Hugh Carton |
| Sgt. Charles S. Abbott | Far. Robert Roulston |
| Cpl. John Tighe | Sad. Henry N. Tucker |
| Cpl. Thomas M. Clarke | Blksm. James A. Chaffee |


PRIVATES


| | |
|---|---|
| Conrad Allbright | William Lee |
| George Allen | John Longrigg |
| James E. Anderson | Reginald A. Loomis |
| William E. Anthon | Franklin A. Maricle |
| Charles R. Appleton | Francis Mayer |
| William E. Baldwin | Hugh McConnell |
| John W. Barrow | Martin M. Moore |
| William Brindley | Henry L. Quinn |
| Edward Bushlepp | Robert Rice |
| Joseph Bennett | John Ritchie |
| Richard F. Chappell (R) | Thomas D. Sanford |
| James Cleveland | Thomas Slater |
| Hugh Curry | Frank Smith |
| John Davis | John H. Smith |
| Michael J. Fitzpatrick | Henry Steiner * |
| Thomas Flood | George Stickney |
| Charles Foster | James Sweeney |
| Joseph Gallagher | John H. Thorison |
| James Galvin | David A. Tilson |
| John W. Hobbs | William Walton |
| Francois Jourdain | Francis A. Wilbur |
| Edward Keeland (R) | William Wilson |
| John Kramer | Frederick Winters |
| Andrew Lee | Edwin D. Wood |


(R) Recruits who joined Column 3 August.
* Wounded 17 June (Battle of Rosebud)

THIRD CAVALRY : COMPANY C


CAPT. FREDERICK VAN VLIET (Comd'g)
1ST LT. ADOLPHUS H. VON LUETTWITZ (Comd'g Co.E
from 28 July)


1st Sgt. William Riley

| | |
|---|---|
| Sgt. John J. Mitchell | Cpl. Eugene Bessiers |
| Sgt. John Manly | Trp. Alfred Helmbold |
| Sgt. John Welsh | Trp. George Steele |
| Cpl. Michael Lanigan (Ill) | Far. William Johnson |
| Cpl. William Stewart | Wag. Henry Wellwood |
| Cpl. Joseph N. Hobsen | Blksm. Heinrich Glucing |


PRIVATES


| | |
|---|---|
| James Allen | William McDonald |
| Henry Bartley | John Miller |
| George W. Bickford | James Mulvey (DS,Wagon Train) |
| Henry Burmeister | James Nolan |
| William B. Dubois | Fred Paul |
| Wentelin Ehrig | James Perkins |
| Perry A. Elden | Frank Quado |
| Walter Gow | John Reed |
| John N. Green | John W. Reppert |
| George Harris (R) | Francis Rodgers |
| William Hart | Louis Sachs |
| William Herd | George E. Sanderson |
| Henry Johnson | John H. Sherman |
| William Larkingland | David O. Sloan (Wagon Train) |
| John D. Leak | John A. Smith |
| Fred Lehman | Harry Snowden |
| Arthur Leroy | Andrew Tierney |
| George P. Lowry | William M. Walcott |
| John Mathews (reduced from | Arnold Weber |
| Saddler 1 August) | Henry Weyworth |
| William P. McCandless | George Williams |
| William J. McClinton | Louis Zinzer |


(R) Recruit joined Column 3 August.

THIRD CAVALRY : COMPANY D

2ND LT. JAMES FERDINAND SIMPSON (Comd'g) *
2ND LT. WILLIAM WALLACE ROBINSON, JR.


1st Sgt. Joseph Robinson

Sgt. Patrick Flood                    Cpl. William Blair
Sgt. John Knox                        Cpl. John McDonald
Sgt. John D. Lindsay                  Cpl. William Ferguson
Sgt. Richard J. McKee                 Cpl. John F. Sanders
Sgt. Charles Taylor                   Trp. Frank Ropetsky (sp)
            Blksm. George W. Hutchinson


PRIVATES


Sidney F. Bates                       Jacob Knittell
Michael Bolton                        James Lown (sick in qtrs)
James Caraley                         John McDonald
Frank Cunningham                      John Miller
Frank DeHaven                         John Phillips
John Delmont                          Charles H. Pullis
John F. Doherty                       Alfero Rawcliffe
August Dorn                           Thomas Riley
Charles Dougherty                     Francis Stahl
John W. Elder                         George Steine
Robert Fisher (R)                     John Stevens
Robert Flint                          Dennis Sullivan
Eugene Jones                          Charles Ward
John H. Kevery (R)(Regt.HQ)           Jacob R. Webb
John Kearney                          Frederick Weber
Thomas Flannery (R)                   J. Franklin Webster
James Kelly                           Thomas C. Whaler (R)(Regt.
            Henry Wielenburg                                    HQ)


* Transferred by Co.B to take command of Co.D, following wounding
        of Capt. Guy V. Henry 17 June (Battle of Rosebud).Capt.
        Henry was removed by wagon train to hospital at Fort
        Fetterman, W.T. 21 June.
(R) Recruits joined Column 3 August.

THIRD CAVALRY : COMPANY E

CAPT. ALEXANDER SUTORIUS *
1ST LT. ADOLPHUS H. VON LUETTWITZ (Comd'g Co.)

1st Sgt. Jeremiah Foley

| | |
|---|---|
| Sgt. Edward Glass | Cpl. Charles N.E. Williams |
| Sgt. Frank P. Secrist | (Ill, Goose Cr.5 Aug.) |
| Sgt. Morgan B. Hawks | Trp. Even S. Worthy |
| Sgt. Joseph Neurohr | Trp. George Hoffstetter |
| Cpl. William Miller | Far. Samuel Stanley |
| Cpl. Edwin F. Ambrose | Sad. Peter Jansen |

Blksm. George Hanernas

PRIVATES

| | |
|---|---|
| Daniel Akley | Bernard Kelly |
| Christopher Ayers | Patrick Kelly |
| John Beattz | John Langan |
| Michael Brannon | Edward Lavelle |
| Joseph Budka | William C.C. Lewis |
| Henry Burton | Thomas Lloyd (Ill,Goose Cr.) |
| William H. Clark | Allen Lupton |
| James Conway | Marcus Magerlein |
| John S. Davis (R) | Edward McKiernan |
| Malachi Dillon (rejoined 4 Aug. | Thomas McNamara |
|   from hosp.,Ft. D.A.Russell) | James Montgomery |
| Richard Dillon | Thomas Nolan |
| Patrick J. Dowling | James H. O'Neil |
| Andrew Dolfer | Joseph Patterson |
| Orlando H. Duren | William Pease |
| Charles F. Eichweitzel | Henry Perkins |
| Thomas Ferguson | James Quinn |
| Lewis S. Grigsby | Alexander Reardon (Goose Cr.) |
| Michael Glannon | William Rice |
| Marcus Hansen | Daniel C. Ross |
| Henry Herald ** | William Schubert |
| William G. Hill(Ill,Goose Cr.) | Patrick Scully |
| Peter Hollen | Alexander Shire |

Daniel Timmey

\* Court-martialed in the field 28 July for being intoxicated while
  Officer of the Guard, and dismissed from the Service. Remained at
  the Goose Creek camp. Von Luettwitz appt. to comd. Co. E.
\*\* Wounded (Battle of Rosebud). In hosp. at Ft. Fetterman 29 June.
(R) Recruit joined Column 3 August.

## THIRD CAVALRY : COMPANY F

1ST LT. ALEXANDER DALLAS BACHE SMEAD (Comd'g)(from 4 August)
2ND LT. BAINBRIDGE REYNOLDS (Temp. comd. to 4 August)

1st Sgt. Michael A. McGann

| | |
|---|---|
| Sgt. Thomas Hackett | Cpl. John Kohn |
| Sgt. John C.A. Warfield(DS:HQ) | Cpl. John Fry |
| Sgt. Robert Emmet | Trp. Arthur N. Chamberlin |
| Sgt. Frank Rugg | Far. Richard O'Grady |
| Sgt. John Gross | Sad. Jeremiah Murphy |
| Cpl. Dennis Giles | Blksm. Averius S. Varney |

### PRIVATES

| | |
|---|---|
| Spencer Bates | Patrick Lynch(R)(Orderly for Regt. Comdr.) |
| Otto Brodersen | Richard Lynch |
| William Chambers(Ill,Goose Cr.) | Michael McGraine |
| David Cochran (R) | Frank McNeal (R) |
| Thomas Cramer | John Meyer |
| Charles Dennis | Jay Mohr (R) |
| Michael T. Donohue | John Murphy |
| Peter Dyke | Alexander Noteman |
| Frank W. Estabrook | Gerold J. O'Grady |
| William Featherly * | Michael O'Hearne |
| Edward Glasheen | Ferdinand Rutten |
| John Hecker | Albert Salice |
| Frederick Hershler | John Semple |
| Julius Jordan | John Staley(Ill,Goose Cr.) |
| Henry Kett | John Tischer |
| John Lannen | Phineas Towne * |
| David Lindsay | Charles R. West |
| Robert Livingston | |

Francis Woltering

(R) Recruits joined Column 3 August.
* Wounded (Battle of Rosebud). In hosp. at Ft. Fetterman 29 June.

## THIRD CAVALRY : COMPANY G

### 1ST LT. EMMET CRAWFORD (Comd'g)

1st Sgt. William Campbell

| | |
|---|---|
| Sgt. Fritz H. Henry | Cpl. Fred Gahlsdorf |
| Sgt. Hugo Deprizin | Trp. Joseph Billow |
| Sgt. William H. Conklin | Trp. Robert McMurray |
| Sgt. William Mason | Far. Patrick Tooel |
| Cpl. Jacob Bender | Blksm. Charles P. Hansen |
| Cpl. Allen J. Rosenberry | Sad. Charles F. Smith |

Wag. Frank McConnell

### PRIVATES

| | |
|---|---|
| Hubert Beohnke | John Martin |
| James H. Bell | James McChesney |
| John B. Comber | John McClain |
| Edward M. Courtney | Edward McCloskey |
| Patrick Delmage | John Miner |
| George M. Edgar | William Moore |
| Frederick P. English | Henry Olsson |
| Byron D. Ferguson | Gotthilf Osterday |
| Henry Ferster | Thomas Phelan |
| Frederick W.S. Fonss | Thomas Quinn |
| Patrick Freeman | Fred Ray |
| James Gandley | James E. Rose |
| Thomas Glanon | Charles W. Ruffle |
| John Hale | Henry Schmidt |
| Edwin Hamilton | Peter Schweikart |
| Jacob Hekel | John Smith |
| Alonzo Hogland | William Smith |
| Adolph Kalber | George Spreight |
| Thomas Kirby | John A. Taylor |
| Edward C. Leitelt | William Taylor |

James Welsh

## THIRD CAVALRY : COMPANY I

CAPT. WILLIAM HOWARD ANDREWS (Comd'g)
1ST LT. ALBERT DOUGLAS KING (joined 14 July; assigned
    Special Duty with Co.B, 4 August)
2ND LT. JAMES EVANS HERON FOSTER


1st Sgt. John Henry

| | |
|---|---|
| Sgt. John Sullivan | Cpl. Frederick Ashwell |
| Sgt. Peter Foster | Cpl. Tobias Carty |
| Sgt. George W. Lowry | Far. Michael O'Rielley |
| Sgt. Andrew Grosh * | Sad. Frank S. Bonnelle |
| Cpl. John I. Byrne | Blksm. Dick C. Kingston |

Blksm. Patrick Pilkington (R)


### PRIVATES

| | |
|---|---|
| Henry Blake | Robert Neel |
| George H. Bowers | James O'Brien * |
| Peter Butler (HQ Orderly) | Robert F. Pratt |
| John Carroll | William Ray |
| John Conley | James Rielley |
| Edward Flood, Jr. | Robert Roberts |
| Frank Hatchcock (Co.Clk.) | Patrick Ryan |
| Benjamin Heald | William Schubert |
| Charles H. Hines | Daniel Shields |
| George Holledered | Lewis Singleton |
| John Hubert | Francis Smith * |
| James M. Hurt | John Smith II |
| Anselm Langman | Fritz Strickert |
| William Leary | Charles W. Stuart * |
| John Losciborski * | Herbert W. Weaver |
| Frank Maginn | Thomas Welch |
| James Martin | William H. West (reduced |
| Michael McMahon |     from Cpl. 20 August) |

Louis Wilmer


(R) Recruit joined Column 3 August.
* Wounded (Battle of Rosebud) 17 June. Hospital (Ft. Fetterman)
  since 29 June.

THIRD CAVALRY : COMPANY L


CAPT. PETER DUMONT VROOM (Comd'g)
2ND LT. GEORGE FRANCIS CHASE


1st Sgt. Joseph Howe

Sgt. Samuel Cook *                          Cpl. Henry J. Bowker
Sgt. Fuller H. Shepperson                       (appt. 1 July)
Cpl. Eugene M. Prince                       Trp. William H. Edwards *
Cpl. Edward Walker                          Trp. Marcellus Goddard
Cpl. David H. Cannell                       Blksm. Charles Webster
Cpl. Otto Tigerstroem                       Far. George B. Oaks
                        Sad. Charles L. Fisk


PRIVATES


Richard Callahan                            James O'Donnell
Christopher Camp                            Louis Phister
Michael Cassidy                             James L. Parks
John Clements                               George Ray
John Creme                                  Antony Schenkberg
William Griffith                            Claud Schmidt
Daniel Harrigan                             John T. Smith
Thomas Hill                                 George A. Soule
Harrison Hincer                             George Sproul
John Kremer *                               Michel Sullivan
Theodore Lowe                               James F. Todd
Fred Mayer                                  Charles Tracy
George H. McDonald                          Azabel R. Van Seer
Charles Miller                              Thomas Walker
Edward Morton (R)                           Richard H. White
Charles Muller (R)                          Rudolph Winn
Thomas F. Norvell                           Alexander Yates


(R) Recruits joined Column 3 August.
* Wounded 17 June (Battle of Rosebud). In hospital at Ft. Fetterman
        by 29 June.

THIRD CAVALRY : COMPANY M


CAPT. ANSON MILLS (Comd'g)
1ST LT. AUGUSTUS CHOTEAU PAUL
2ND LT. FREDERICK SCHWATKA


1st Sgt. Franklin B. Robinson (appt.7 August)

| | |
|---|---|
| Sgt. Frank V. Erhard | Cpl. Myron P. Boyce (R) |
| Sgt. Alexander B. Ballard | (appt.7 August) |
| Sgt. John A. Kirkwood (appt.7 Aug.) | Cpl. Peter L. Hogeboom |
| Sgt. Gilbert Exford (appt. 7 Aug.) | Trp. Elmer A. Snow * |
| (Ill, Goose Creek) | Trp. Frank Serfas |
| Cpl. Mathew Grappenstetter | Blksm. Albert Glawinski |

Sad. Charles H. Lindenberg


PRIVATES


| | |
|---|---|
| Henry Badgery | Albert Morganthaler |
| John H. Boyce | Jeremiah Murphy |
| Carlos L. Chamberlin | Thomas I. O'Keefe |
| Bernard F. Cullen | Adam Pringle |
| Henry E. Curley | George Raab |
| Bernard Diringer | Dave C. Renear |
| John E. Douglass | William H. Reynolds |
| Isaac S. Drake | Blaseus Schmalz |
| Dennis B. Duggan | Joseph Schmidtt |
| George Foster | Fred Schuttle |
| John A. Foster | James Shanley |
| Isaac J. Kelton | George Sheehan (R) |
| Dennis W. Larkin | John W. Singer |
| Patrick I. Maguire | Robert Smith |
| Hugh H. Massy | John I. Stevenson |
| Timothy McCarthy | John Sweeney |
| William McGinniss | Charles E. Tredick |
| James B. Miller | Soren O. Very |
| Joseph W. Morgan | Joseph Walzer |


(R) Recruits joined Column 3 August.
* Wounded 17 June (Battle of Rosebud); taken to hospital in Fort
  Fetterman by 29 June.

INFANTRY BATTALION COMMAND


MAJOR ALEXANDER CHAMBERS (4th Inf.) (Comd'g)
1ST LT. THADDEUS HURLBUT CAPRON (Co.C. 9th Inf.),Adjutant


FOURTH INFANTRY

COMPANY D : CAPT. AVERY BILLINGS CAIN
            1ST LT. HENRY SETON

COMPANY F : CAPT. GERHARD LUKE LUHN
            2ND LT. SATTERLEE CLARK PLUMMER (attached 4 Aug.)

COMPANY G : CAPT. WILLIAM HENRY POWELL
            2ND LT. ALBERT BURNLEY CRITTENDEN


NINTH INFANTRY

COMPANY C : CAPT. SAMUEL MUNSON
            2ND LT. HAYDEN DELANY

COMPANY G : CAPT. THOMAS BREDIN BURROWES
            1ST LT. WILLIAM LEWIS CARPENTER

COMPANY H : CAPT. ANDREW SHERIDAN BURT
            2ND LT. EDGAR BROOKS ROBERTSON
            2ND LT. CHARLES MORTIMER ROCKEFELLER


FOURTEENTH INFANTRY

COMPANY B : CAPT. JAMES KENNINGTON
            2ND LT. CHARLES FREDERICK LLOYD

COMPANY C : CAPT. DANIEL WEBSTER BURKE
            1ST LT. JOHN MURPHY (Co.B) (attached)

COMPANY F : CAPT. THOMAS FRY TOBEY
            2ND LT. FREDERICK SANSCAY CALHOUN

COMPANY I : 1ST LT. FRANK TAYLOR
            2ND LT. RICHARD THOMAS YEATMAN

FOURTH INFANTRY : COMPANY D


CAPT. AVERY BILLINGS CAIN *
1ST LT. HENRY SETON (Comd'g)


1st Sgt. Ruben P. Dexter **

Sgt. Joseph Lister **              Cpl. Alfred F. Funk
Sgt. Bernard Degnan               Cpl. Thomas Conboy
Sgt. Smith Chittenden             Trp. Alfred Smith
Sgt. John F. Cochrane             Trp. James Connelly
                    Art. Charles McMahon


PRIVATES


John Benazet                      John Kail
Charles R. Bill                   Leon Lawrence
John H. Bishop                    August Lehn (R)
George W. Bowley                  Gilbert Long
John T. Bowman (R)                Thomas Maher
William G. Clark (R)              Daniel McCormack
Monroe Cole                       William Perry
Richard F. Colter (R)             Charles Reid (R)
Carl Dahlman                      Frank Rivers (R)
Peter Decker                      John W. Sandy (R)
Timothy Deily (R)                 Lawrence Schneiderhan
James Devlin                      Joshua Scott
David F. Dowling                  Rhinehart Smith (R)
John Edwards                      Franklin A. Smith (R)
Louis Eiskamp                     John Stinger (R)
Bernard Elsenheimer (R)           Charles Stollnow
Richard Flynn                     Richard Taylor (R)
Philip George                     Albert Wagner
Richard Harney                    James Wells (R)
Irving Heaslip                    Augustus Thilman (R)
Patrick Higerty                   Edward Williams


(R) Recruits joined Column 3 August.
* Ordered to Omaha 23 August 1876 for "insanity", Lieut. Seton
  comd'g Co. since 4 August, prior to which date and following
  Cain had been evidencing symptoms of the unbalanced mind. However,
  Cain managed to remain with the Co. until Column reached Yellowstone River 17 Augustm and was then ordered aboard the 'Carroll'
  for the return to Omaha.
** Dexter relieved as 1st Sgt. 29 July, and Lister appt. and serving
  until Dexter reappointed 1st Sgt. on 10 August.

FOURTH INFANTRY : COMPANY F


CAPT. GERHARD LUKE LUHN (Comd'g)
2ND LT. SATTERLEE CLARK PLUMMER (Attached 4 August) *


1st Sgt. John D. O'Brien
Sgt. George W. Rowsell            Cpl. John C. Cain
Cpl. Ludwig Roper                 Cpl. Lucius E. Stearns
Cpl. George Wood                  Musc. Peter Cassidy
           Artif. Jay E. Brandow


PRIVATES


Frederick Albertson (R)          William E. Helvia
Oscar Baker                      August J. Helzer (R)
John Baptiste                    William Johnston
Joseph Biggs (R)                 Patrick Kane (R)
George Bloomingdale              William Kent
Oliver F. Browden                Christopher Larsen
Edward Buird                     Patrick Lonargan
Alexander N. Campbell (R)        David Meserole
James Conklin (R)                John McCarty
Michael Conlon (R)               Patrick McEnery
Michael Cunningham               Richard O'Sullivan
Robert Dickson                   George Rehberg
Lawrence Dugan (R)               Joseph B. Rozell (R)
James Ferguson                   Oscar Sloan
William Frisby (DS,Goose Creek)  William Stilwell
John Gallagher                   William Swain
Samuel Godfrey (R)               Jacob Schumaker
William Green                    Frederick Taska
August Gunker                    Joseph Turner
John Healey                      James White (R)
           William E. Wolfe


(R) Recruits joined Column 3 August.
* Special Field Orders, No.22.

## FOURTH INFANTRY : COMPANY G

CAPT. WILLIAM HENRY POWELL (Comd'g)
2ND LT. ALBERT BURNLEY CRITTENDEN

1st Sgt. Conrad Bahr

| | |
|---|---|
| Sgt. Joseph A. Turner | Cpl. Jacob Koch |
| Sgt. Rochus Schalgen | Cpl. August Miller |
| Sgt. Charles H. McFarland | Cpl. Calvin Kusbaum |
| Sgt. Henry Shields | Cpl. Richard G. Gregg |

Musc. Frank Dubern

### PRIVATES

| | |
|---|---|
| Francis M. Avey | Peter Meagher |
| Herman Braunsdorf | John Miller |
| Henry F. Brown | James C. Monroe |
| Robert Brown | Charles Morgan |
| John Cannon (QM Dept.,Goose Cr.) | James A. Morton |
| Joseph W. Copley | Henry Mosher |
| Edward Crouch | Samuel D. Peters |
| William Cullen | Christopher T. Reilley |
| William Davis | Isaac Richner |
| Jack C. Deats | John Sheridan |
| Dennis Dooley | George Smith |
| Owen Fitzpatrick | Anthony Smolinski |
| William Ford | Basil S. Spangler |
| Henry Foster | John Speckman |
| George Gesell | Charles W. Starke |
| Bernhard Kramer | Stephen S. Viele |
| James L. Krone (Ill,Goose Creek) | Richard M. Whelan |

Thomas J. Wiggins

## NINTH INFANTRY : COMPANY C

CAPT. SAMUEL MUNSON (Comd'g)
1ST LT. THADDEUS HURLBUT CAPRON (Appointed
 Infantry Battalion Adjutant 3 July)
2ND LT. HAYDEN DELANY (joined Column 13 July)


                    1st Sgt. James Whelan
Sgt. Stephen Malloy               Cpl. Andrew Murphy
Sgt. William W. Butler            Cpl. George Kreissig
Sgt. Jesse H. Farmer              Cpl. William S. Parsons
Cpl. Marshall Crocker             Trp. Antonio Blitz(Goose Cr.)
                  Artif. William H. Smith


### PRIVATES

Sylvester Blanwelt                Julius Happi
Howard Boyer                      Solomon Hirschberg
Edward Burns                      Thomas Hughes
James W. Butler                   Samuel Hunt
William B. Colcroft               Samuel Jacob
Harley Crittenden                 Andrew Johnson
Michael Deegan                    Daniel Mahoney
Christopher Dillon                George W. McAnuity
Edward Donnelly                   Hugh McLean
Michael Dougherty                 Ernest Melin
John C. Eisenberg                 Henry Mell
Charles Elward                    Oliver Navarre
Barney Flanagan                   Charles A. Nichols
Samuel Gibson                     Calvin Ramsome
Thomas W. Granberry               Walter C. Smith
Frank Hamill                      Ole Tothamer
Frederick Hanshammer              Luther B. Wolfe
                  Albert Zimmerman

NINTH INFANTRY : COMPANY G


CAPT. THOMAS BREDIN BURROWES (Comd'g) (to 24 Aug.) *
1ST LT. WILLIAM LEWIS CARPENTER (Comd'g after 24 Aug.) *


1st Sgt. John C. Rafferty

| | |
|---|---|
| Sgt. Francis Doyle | Cpl. Rudolph Ormann |
| Sgt. Frederick Klein | Cpl. Joseph S. Wrisley |
| Sgt. Frank McCarthy | Trp. William Doody |
| Cpl. James Delaney | Trp. Hugh Thomson |
| Cpl. Timothy O'Sullivan | Artif. Joseph Holtz |


PRIVATES


| | |
|---|---|
| John Anderson | August Hocksmith |
| William Calahan (R) | Theodore L. Johnson (R) |
| John Campbell (R) | Barney Keife (R) |
| Richard L. Case | Frederick Lafine |
| Edwin Chenerwirth (R) | John C. Lee (R) |
| Edward Conlin | Alexander M. Lowrie |
| Thomas Dunivan (R) | Michael Murphy |
| Patrick Dwyer | John G. Newman |
| William Ecrestein | John Norton |
| William Faulman | Cornelius Reardon (R) |
| James Gaskill | Frank Shurhammer (R) |
| William E. Glick(Ill,Goose Cr.) | Charles S. Slocum (R) |
| Zachery Y. Guy (R) | Samuel Smith(Ill,Goose Cr.) |
| William R. Hardin | John Thomas(Ill,Goose Cr.) |
| Michael Healey | Charles W. Wilson |
| Harvey Henery (R) | Samuel H. Woolen |
| Thomas W. Hiram (R) | Samuel C. Wynkoop |

Rudolph Zysset


(R) Recruits joined Column 3 August.
* Burrowes released from comd. 24 August for Special Duty in charge
  of returning the disabled and sick on the 'Carroll' to Bismarck
  and other hospital locations. Carpenter would assume Comd. of Co.G.

## NINTH INFANTRY : COMPANY H

CAPT. ANDREW 'ANDY' SHERIDAN BURT (Comd'g)
2ND LT. EDGAR BROOKS ROBERTSON
2ND LT. CHARLES MORTIMER ROCKEFELLER (Attached 4 Aug.)


### 1st Sgt. August Lange

Sgt. Henry Stoll                    Cpl. John McFarlane
Sgt. Charles F. Miller              Cpl. Sylvester Poole
Sgt. Danford R. Langley             Trp. Bernhard Bloemer
Sgt. John Smith                     Trp. Julius Pernell


### PRIVATES

Louis Allison (DS,Goose Cr.)        John McCann
John H. Atwood                      John McCormick
Uriah Baker (R)                     August Metz (R)
Joseph S. Bennett                   James Morgan
Charles Beyschlag                   William Nobles
Samuel B. Brown                     Richard O'Hearn
James Chilson (R)                   Daniel P. Reddy
George Coy                          Max Riech
James Duffy (R)                     John Seery
David N. Eshelman                   Aaron Smith
Robert Fitz Henry                   George S. Spurgeon (R)
Robert Gardner (R)                  John Stephenson
Philip H. Gatz (R)                  Warren Taylor
Luther C. Hagerty (R)               John Walsh
Thaddeus N. Hendricksen             Michael Walsh
Frank Lalande (R)                   James Waters
George E. Leggatt                   Peter Winegardner
James Lyons (R)                     William Wood (R)
                    Wilson Zurmehly (R)


(R) Recruits joined Column 3 August.

FOURTEENTH INFANTRY : COMPANY B


CAPT. JAMES KENNINGTON (Comd'g)
2ND LT. CHARLES FREDERICK LLOYD
1ST LT. JOHN MURPHY (Attached to Co.C)


1st Sgt. Frank King

| | |
|---|---|
| Sgt. Robert Quidde | Cpl. William K. Hudson |
| Sgt. Howard G. Furman | Cpl. Francis S. Niles |
| Sgt. Alfred Seadorf | Cpl. Benjamin F. Williams |
| Sgt. Joseph Hornick | Trp. Charles Baker |

Trp. William B. Kennedy


PRIVATES


| | |
|---|---|
| Albert Bird | Charles H. Forborg |
| Thomas J. Blake | Patrick Hanley(Ill,24 Aug.) |
| Henry J. Boney | Samuel S. Hawkins(Ft.Fetterman) |
| Charles Borden | Henry Hayes |
| William Brown | David Henden |
| Philip Buckert | Henry Hinternesch |
| Howard Bullman (R) | Joseph Horton |
| Joseph Burget | Charles McPartlen |
| Martin Cuddy | George Miller |
| John Curtis | Charles Mohrenstein |
| James Croley (R) | Edward Morton |
| George W. Davis | Peter Nolan |
| John Desmond | Delos Ransom |
| Thomas Donley | Herbert S. Rich |
| George W. Earls | Thomas Russell |
| Frank Farnham | Charles Senni (R) |
| Lemis Fassold | John Smith |

Peter Till (Ill,24 Aug.Yellowstone R.)


(R) Recruits joined Column 3 August.

FOURTEENTH INFANTRY : COMPANY C


CAPT. DANIEL WEBSTER BURKE (Comd'g)
1ST LT. JOHN MURPHY (Co.B) (attached)


1st Sgt. Francis Gallagher

Sgt. Miles Doran                    Cpl. Thomas Jones
Sgt. Louis Bardy                    Cpl. William Baumgarten
Sgt. Samuel P. Spalding             Cpl. Alford G. Woodwell
Sgt. William W. Jordan              Musc. Frank Louis
Cpl. Cornelius Shea                 Musc. Robert A. Bain


PRIVATES

Edward Bohl                         Charles Keenan
James B. Burns                      Thomas Leech
Patrick Burns                       Augustus Lipthar
Thomas Clayton                      John Meason
John Cogan                          Herman Mendel
Mathew Collins                      Edward L. Murphy
Thomas Connerton                    Matthew Nolan
Gottlieb Dammel                     James Radcliff
David H. Decker                     Thaddeus Robinson
Frederick Diehr                     John Rosenburger(Ill,Goose Cr
Junius Edwards                      James M. Sullivan
Ambrose Gaghagan                    Lewis Thomas
James Goss                          John Volker(Ill,Ft.Fetterman)
John W. Hall                        George B. Wait
Otis W. Hiveley                     William Waterhouse
John J. Jordan                      John A. Weeks


(Attached to Co.C)


Mathew Flood (Absent:Ill)          John Lonagan
            Abraham Montieth


(Discharged)


Frank Gentzer (1 August 1876)

FOURTEENTH INFANTRY : COMPANY F


CAPT. THOMAS FRY TOBEY (Comd'g)
2ND LT. FREDERICK SANSCAY CALHOUN


1st Sgt. Patrick McAleer

Sgt. John Bourke            Cpl. James Allen
Sgt. Edward Kelly           Cpl. George L. Lurnbreger
Sgt. Joseph McClanahan      Cpl. Michael McLaughlin


PRIVATES


Benjamin Black              Julius Herbert
Charles Brown               John Karche
Patrick Burke               Thomas Knight
William M. Chambers         George Kolby
Robert Cleave               George Lewis
Bernard Creamer             Con McGee
James Daly                  Robert Moore (Ill,Goose Cr.)
Marcus Dame                 Christopher Mullins
Barnum Doan (R)             Charles A. Pool
Joseph Dunnigan (R)         Michael Quinlaw (R)
Jacob Eath                  William H. Revenew
Jacob J. Ehred              Frank Ruiz
Jacob Flohn                 Bernard Samuel
Aaron B. Foster             Albion R. Strang
John B. Gauruaurd (sp)      George T. Strang
William Gentles             George T. Stacy
                William Taylor
                Conrad Ziltle


(R) Recruits joined Column 3 August.

FOURTEENTH INFANTRY : COMPANY I

1ST LT. FRANK TAYLOR (Comd'g)
2ND LT. RICHARD THOMAS YEATMAN

1st Sgt. Cornelius Barrett

| | |
|---|---|
| Sgt. Paul Kelliher | Cpl. William H. Scribner |
| Sgt. William T. Caselton | Cpl. Otto Dangeleson |
| Cpl. Ernest L. McAdams | Musc. Henry Bernard |
| Cpl. John K. Zimmerman | Musc. Thomas O'Sullivan |
| | (dischgd 3 Aug.) |

PRIVATES

| | |
|---|---|
| Andrew Ackerman | Henry Lies |
| William R. Barrett(Ill,Goose Cr.) | Dennis Lynch (R) |
| John Bartley | Eugene Matcher * |
| Terence Cullen | James M. Moore |
| Joseph Derush (R) | Maxmilian Moushart |
| Jerome A. Ellrich | Denis Mullane |
| Edward Emerson | Ben Murphy |
| John J. Fussner | Michael O'Brien |
| Herman Feil (R) | Philip Rintz (R) |
| Patrick M. Gibbons | Mathew Rielly |
| Wendel Hagdorn (R) | Andrew Shields |
| John T. Hill | John Smith |
| James Holden | Frank Spearman |
| Thomas Hulohan | William Stevens |
| James Johnston | John Strut |
| Patrick Kelly (R) | George Tyler |
| Stephen Leonard | Harry Van Houton |
| Charles Liel | Charles Waugh |

(R) Recruits joined Column 3 August.
* Ill on steamer 'Carroll', Yellowstone River, 20 August.

THE SIBLEY SCOUT : JULY 6 - 9, 1876

2ND LT. FREDERICK WILLIAM SIBLEY (Co.E, 2nd Cav.) (Comd'g)

COMPANY A (2nd Cav.)

1st Sgt. Gregory P. Harrington

Pvt. William L. Regan          Pvt. Daniel Munger
Pvt. Hugh Green                Pvt. George B. Robinson

COMPANY B (2nd Cav.)

Sgt. Charles W. Day

Pvt. Henry G. Collins          Pvt. Patrick Hasson
Pvt. Charles F. Edwards        Pvt. William A. Hills

COMPANY D (2nd Cav.)

Sgt. Oscar Cornwall

Pvt. James Darcey              Pvt. George A. Stone
Pvt. Samuel W. Hone            Pvt. Joseph Ward

COMPANY E (2nd Cav.)

Sgt. William P. Cooper

Pvt. William I. Croley         Pvt. Valentine Rufus
Pvt. William J. Dougherty      Pvt. Jacob Heird

COMPANY I (2nd Cav.)

Cpl. Thomas C. Marrion

Pvt. Martin Maher              Pvt. George Watts
Pvt. George Rhode              Pvt. Hermann Ashkey

(SCOUTS)

Baptiste 'Big Bat' Pourier          Frank Grouard

(OTHERS)

Correspondent John F. Finerty (Chicago Times)
Packer John Becker ('Jim Traynor' or 'Trailer Jack')

A

Abbott, Charles 62
Abbott, Charles S.73
Abbott, Jas. D. 7
Abbotts, Harry 33
Abel, Geo. 48
Abrams, Wm. G. 39
Ackerman, Andrew 92
Ackerman, Chas. 38
Ackison, David 33
Acres, Wm. 46
ADAM, EMIL 55, 58
Adams, Chas. 51
Adams, Chas. H. 24
Adams, Harvey 63
Adams, Jacob 36
Adams, Jas. 16
Adams, Jas. A. 43
Adams, John W. 56
Adams, Patrick 56
Ahab, Mathias 49
Ahern, John 49
Ahrens, Christian59
Ainger, Francis 41
Ainley, Jas. 57
Aischiff, Wm. 64
Akers, Jas. 35    .
Akley, Daniel 76
Alberts, Chas. 6
Alberts, Jas. H.32
Albertson, Fred.84
Albrecht, Alex. 67
Alcorn, Frank 44
Alcott, Sam. 29
Aller, Chas. 29
Alex, Aion(?)63
Alexander, Ed. 21
Allbright, Conrad73
Allbring, Thos.65
Allen, Eugene 53
Allen, Frank 50
Allen, Fred. 14
Allen, Geo. 73
Allen, Jas. 72
Allen, Jas. 74
Allen, Jas. 91
Allen, Robt.H.44
Aller, Chas.29
Aller, Chas.N.56
Allison, Louis 88
Allspach, Chris.15
Almon, Chas.F.20
Alten, John G.68
Amart, Louis 49
Amart, Rudolph 49

Ambrose, Edwin F.76
Ameling, Henry 52
Ames, Cornelius 57
Anderson, Adam A.50
Anderson, Alex. 14
Anderson, Chas.72
Anderson, Henry 58
Anderson, Jas.E.73
Anderson, John 48
Anderson, John 72
Anderson, John 87
Anderson, Robt. 43
Andresor, John 39
Andrews, John 49
ANDREWS, WM.H.66,79
Angus, Chas. 67
Anthon, Wm.E.73
Anthony, Jas.69
Applegate, F.R.15
Appleton, Chas.R.73
Archer, Edson F.39
Armsbury, John 57
Armstrong, Jas.18
Armstrong, Wm.J.72
Arndt, Otto 26
Arnold, Ben 54
Arnold, Sylvester65
Arold, Ernest 59
Arthur, Chas. 53
Artmoin, John A.63
Ascough, John B.32
Ashkey,Herman71,93
Ashton, Isaiah(Dr.)2
Ashwall, Fred. 79
Atkinson, John F.15
Atcheson, Robt.D.22
Atwood, John H.88
Auberg, Jacob 64
Aubrey, Wm.H.8
Aughey, Thos.68
Austin, Chas.67
Austin, Daniel 68
Austin, Frank 50
Avey, Francis M.85
Avrey, Chas.E.36
Ayers, Chris. 76


B

Baader, Lee 70
Baaer, John 9
Babcock, Wm. 72
Beccehh, Chas.E.59

BACHE,ALFRED B.55,61
Backer, Franz 59
Backer,Heinrich 65
Backer, John 51
Backer, Louis 45
Backman, Fred.53
Badgery, Henry 81
Bagley, Geo. 48
Bahr, Conrad 85
Baiggo, Thos.9
Bailey, John E.30
Bailey, Richard 42
Bain, Robt.A.90
Bainbridge,Henry43
Baird, Wm. 50
Baker, Chas. 89
Baker, Conrad 72
Baker, John 34
Baker, John 43
Baker, Jos. 14
Baker, Oscar 84
Baker, (scout) 2
BAKER, STEPHEN 1,18
Baker, Thos. 62
Baker, Uriah 88
Baker, Wm. 6
Bakovsky, John 57
BALDWIN, FRANK D.47
Baldwin, Wm.E. 73
BALL, EDWARD 4,16
Ballard, Alex.B.81
Bamford, Jas.M.59
Bancroft, Neil 29
Bane, John 12
Bang, Frank F. 19
Banks, Chas. 39
Banse, John 55
Baptiste, John 84
Barbour. (Dr.) 2
Bardy, Louis 90
Barker, Albert E.62
Barker, Chas. A.10
Barkman, Jos. 11
Barmetter, Jacob 59
Barnaby, Geo.E. 15
Barnes, Geo. H. 6
Barnett, Harvey 52
Barney, Chas. 26
Barney, John 41
Barre, Lewis M. 58
Barrett, Cornelius 92
Barrett, Thos. 61
Barrett, Wm.R. 92

B

Barringer, Frank 63
Barrow, John W. 73
Barrowman, Jas. 48
Barry, Peter O. 2,30
Barsantee, Jas. F.30
Barteman, Julius 53
Bartholf, Jas. F. 29
Bartlett, Fred. 72
Bartley, Henry 74
Bartley, John 48
Bartley, John 92
Baster, Wm. 53
Bates, Hugh 43
Bates, Jos. 40
Bates, Sidney F.75
Bates, Spencer 77
Batterall, Darian20
Battey, Wilbur H.51
Bauer, Oscar 51
Bauman, Herman 63
Baumbach, Conrad 26
Baumgarten, Wm. 90
Baumgartner, Louis29
Bauer, Chris. 52
Bauer, Jacob 38
Bauer, John 46
Bayer, Edward 51
Bayles, Frank 58
Beary, Geo.C. 10
Beatty, Jas. 51
Beaver, Wm.S. 24
Beble, Geo.H.53
Bechinor, Robt.49
Beck, Benj. 26
Beck, Fred. 50
Becker, Chas. 19
Becker, Chas. 5
Becker, John 93
Beckham, Lindsey59
Beckman, Chas. 20
Beckman, Geo.W.60
Begley, Edward 2
Belged, John 44
Bell, Jas. 12
Bell, Jas. 10
Bell, Jas. 10
Bell, Jas. H. 78
Bellows, Richard49
Benazet, John 83
Bendell, Wm.D. 10
Bender, August W.7
Bender, Fred. 36
Bender, Henry 39

Bender, Jacob 78
BENNETT,ANDREW S. 3,
            47,48
Bennett John O. 6
Bennett, Jos. 73
Bennett, Jos. S. 88
Benson, Jas. D. 39
Benson, Wm. 16
BENTEEN, WM. FRED.4,
            28,36
Benton, Arthur 58
Bernard, Henry 92
Berncisco, Albert46
Bernhardt, Fred.59
Berwald, Frank 33
Bessey, Chas.A.72
Bessiers, Eugene 74
Betts, Benj. 14
Beverly, Jas. 16
Beyschlag, Chas. 88
Biarly, Jas. 20
Bickford, Geo.M.71
Bickford, Geo.W.74
Biddle, Jos. 11
Bidwell, Chas. 62
Bidwell, Philander
                62
Bigalsky, Gottlieb
                72
Biggs, Jos.S. 84
Bigman, Frank 49
Bill, Chas. R. 83
Billow, Jos. 78
Bills, Wm.A. 72
Binderald, Herman
                40
Binkhoff Herman20
Birach, Chas. 18
Bird, Albert 89
Bird, Benj.F. 60
Birns, Chas. 1,25
Bisbing, Jas. 22
Bischoff, Chas.H.
                31
Bishley, Henry P.36
Bishop, Chas. 12
BISHOP, HOEL SMITH
            55,62
Bishop, John H. 83
Bixby, Herbert 15
Black, Amos 71
Black, Benj. 91
Blackwood, Robt.72

Blair, Jas. 38
Blair, Wilbur F. 29
Blair, Wm. 75
Blake, Henry 79
Blake, Mathew 63
Blake, Thos. 29
Blake, Thos.J. 89
Blanwell, Sylvester86
Blaut, Jakob 63
Blitz, Antonio 86
Blohm, Augustus 53
Bloemer, Bernhard 88
Bloomingdale, Geo.84
Blunt, Geo. 38
Boam, Wm. 30
Boch, John 70
Bockerman, August 26
Boehnke, Hubert 78
Boen, Thos F. 21
Boggs, Jas.A. 73
Bohl, Edward 90
Bohner, Aloys 32
Boissen, Chris. 38
Boland, Edward 62
Boles, Jas. 1
Bolling, Fred. 49
Bolton, Michael 75
Bolton, Wm. 20
Bolts, Wm. 11
Bond, Edward 62
Bond, Fred. G. 20
Boney, Henry J. 89
Bonnelle, Frank S.79
Boone, Lewis C. 58
BOOTH, CHAS. A. 9
Booth, Wm.H. 50
Borden, Chas. 89
Boren, A. 30
Borie, Louis 50
Bosquill, Patrick 12
Boss, Chas. 44
Bott, Geo. 29
Boucher, Henry 43
Bouger, Jos. 31
Bounsall, Wm.C. 58
Bourke, Henry M. 65
Bourke, John 91
BOURKE, JOHN GREGORY 54
Bovard, Jas. 5
Bower, Fred. 63
Bowers, Geo.A. 51
Bowers, Geo. H.79
Bowker, Henry J. 80

B

Bowley, Geo.W. 83
Bowman, John J. 23
Bowman, John T. 83
Boyce, John H. 81
Boyce, Myron P. 81
Boyd, Henry 53
Boyer, Howard 86
Boyer, Irwin L. 52
Boyle, Jas. 42
Boyle, Jas. P.35
Boyle, Jos. 72
Boyle, Patrick 24
Bradeen, Sam. 59
Brading, Thos.J.48
Bradley, Elmore 23
BRADLEY, JAS. H. 7
Bradley, Jos. 61
Bradley, Patrick 63
Brady, Chas. 41
Brady, Jas. 49
Brady, Patrick 31
Brady, Thos. 60
Brady, Wm. 49
Brainard, Geo.30
Branagan, Jas. 67
Brandle, Wm. 31
Brandow, Jay E.84
Brannigan, John 50
Brannon, Michael 76
Branshoop, John 57
Brant, Abram B. 32
Brass, Wm. 62
Braun, Franz C.37
Braunsdorf,Herman
                85
Breed, Wm.H. 59
Breen, Peter 44
Bremer, Henry 63
Brenenstuhl,Sam.51
Brennan, John 31
Brereton, Edward 44
Breshnahan,Maurice
                72
Bresnahan,Cornelius
                38
Brierly, Jas. 20
Briggs, Geo. 41
Brindley, Wm. 73
Bringes, John 29
Brinkerhoff,Henry35
Brinkman, Wm. 18
BRISBIN, JAS.SANKS4
Brockmeyer, Wesley2

Brodersen, Otto 77
Broderick, Jos. 22
Broderick, Thos. 62
Brogan, Jos. 52
Brogerri, Antonio 67
Bromwell, Latrobe 33
Brophey, John 48
Brooking, John D. 50
Brooks, Henry 52
Brooks, Wm.J. 52
Browden, Oliver F.84
Brown, Albert E. 18
Brown, Alex. 35
Brown, Anton 60
Brown, Chas. 30
Brown, Chas. 91
Brown, Daniel 62
Brown, Edwin M.47,48
Brown, Frank J. 62
Brown, Henry 48
Brown, Henry 29
Brown, Henry F. 85
Brown, Hiram E. 34
Brown, Jas. 30
Brown, John 16
Brown, Jos. 38
Brown, Lorenzo D.8
Brown, Nathan J. 39
Brown, Robt. 85
Brown, Samuel B. 88
Brown, Sanford F. 19
Brown, Wm. 89
Brown, Wm. H. 22
Brown, Wm. H. 53
Bryan, Michael 56
Bryant, Robt. 37
BUBB, JOHN WILSON 54
Bubenheim,Konrad 17
Bucher, Richard 36
Buckert, Philip 89
Buckles, Thos. 42
Buckley, Wm. 18
Buckminster,Richard
                60
Budka, Jos. 76
Buggle, Michael 24
Buird, Edward 84
Bullen, Jas. 48
Bullman, Howard 89
Bullock, Chas. 42
Bunger, Chas. 63
Burbach, Nicholas70
Burdeff, Peter G.21

Burdick. Benj. 26
Burdick. Frank C. 58
Burgdorf, Chas. 38
Burget, Jos. 89
Burgess, Wm. H. 53
Burgo, Henry 42
BURKE, DANIEL WEBSTER
                82.90
Burke, Edmund H. 38
Burke, Patrick 91
Burke, Richard 51
Burke, Thos. J. 51
Burke, Ulrich 34
Burke, Wm. 14
Burke, Wm. W. 69
Burkett, John W. 33
Burkhardt, Chas. 38
Burkman, John 39
Burleigh, Walter 1
Burlis, Edmond 26
Burmeister, Henry 74
Burnett,Cornelius 58
BURNETT, LEVI F. 5
Burnett, Phillip 71
Burns, Chas. 30
Burns, Edward 86
Burns, Jas. B. 90
Burns, Jas. H. 52
Burns, John 10
Burns, Patrick 90
Burns, Peter 37
Burns, Thos. H. 39
BURROWES, THOS. BREDIN
                82,87
BURT, ANDREW SHERIDAN
                82,88
Burton, Henry 76
Bury, Berthold 43
Busch, Jacob 57
Busch, Louis 53
Bushlepp, Edward 73
Buskirk, John H. 11
Buskirk, Stephen O. 33
Butler, Henry P. 57
Butler, Jas. 49
Butler, Jas. W. 34
Butler, Jas. W. 86
Butler, John 61
Butler, Peter 79
Butler, Wm. 20
Butler, Wm. W. 86
Butterly, Matthew 10
Butterworth,Wm. H. 67

B

Buttner, Leopold 65
Bwaver, Oliver H.63
BYRNE, BERNARD A.22
Byrne, John I. 79

C

Caddle, Michael 37
Cahill, James 41
CAIN, AVERY B.82,83
Cain, Morris 40
Cain, John C. 84
Cainwell, Frank 61
Calahan, Wm. 87
Caldwell, Wm. 30
CALHOUN, FRED.S.82,
              91
Callaghan,Richard51
Callahan,Richard 80
Callan, Jas 30
Callan, Thos.J.30
Calnon, Simon 64
Cameron, Jas. 18
Campbell, Alex. 84
Campbell, Chas.A.30
Campbell,David 1
Campbell,Henry C.67
Campbell,Jeremiah38
Campbell, John 87
Campbell, Wm. 78
CAMPBELL, WM.J.46
Caniff, Jas. 64
Cannell, David 80
Canning,Mathew 5
Cannon, John 85
Capes, Wm. 40
Capron, E.R. 48
CAPRON,THADDEUS H.
              82,86
Caraley, Jas. 75
Cardinal,Julius65
Carey, Jas.H. 69
Carey, Michael F.33
CARLAND, JOHN 18
Carland, Wm.W. 1
Carlin, Edward 43
Carmody, Thos. 30
Carnahan,Robt.A.63
Carney, Jas. 60
Carney, Thos.16
Carpenter,Alfred W.
              58
Carpenter,Edward49

CARPENTER, WM.L.82,87
CARR,EUGENE ASA 55
Carr, John A. 67
Carroll, Andrew 63
Carroll, Daniel 30
Carroll, Jas. 16
Carroll, John 16
Carroll, John 59
Carroll, John 79
Carroll, Jos. 26
Carroll, Michael 58
Carroll, Thos. 14
Carry, John J. 30
Carson, Wm. 6
Carsten, Hans 50
Carter, Andrew 26
CARTER,MASON 3,47,53
Carton, Hugh 73
Carty,George C.48
Carty, Tobias 79
Cary, Jas.C. 58
Case,Richard L.87
Caselton, Wm.T.92
Casey,Cornelius 53
CASEY,EDWARD W.42
Casey, John 20
Casey, Timothy 62
Casey, Wm.C. 60
Cashman, John 9
Cassidy, Jas. 51
Cassidy, John H.25
Cassidy,Michael 80
Cassidy, Peter 84
Catarious, John 58
Causby, Thos. 26
Cecil, Wm.H. 22
Chaffee, Jas.A. 73
Chaffin, Wm.H. 56
Chamberlain,Albert
              65
Chamberlain,Jas.A.
              15
Chamberlin,Arthur N.
              77
Chamberlin,Carlos L.
              81
Chamberlin,Geo.H.34
CHAMBERS, ALEX.82
Chambers, Henry 68
Chambers, Wm. 77
Chambers, Wm.M. 91
CHANCE, JOSIAH 20
Channell, Wm. 36

Chaplin, Lewis 12
Chapman,E.Dwight 14
Chapman,Ernest H.57
Chapman, Wm.H. 33
Chapman, Wm.W. 26
Chappel, Henry 56
Chappell,Richard F.
              73
CHASE,GEO.FRANCIS 66
Chase, John C. 17
Chenerwirth,Edwin 87
Chesterwood, Chas.38
Chilson, Jas. 88
Chittenden,Smith 83
Cigan, Patrick 15
Clancy,Michael M.39
Clanton, Jos.S. 57
Clarison,Peter F.24
Clarkins, John J.6
Clark,Elbert (Dr.)2
Clark, Frank 30
Clark, Herbert 9
Clark, Howard 13
Clark, Jas. 18
Clark, John 16
Clark, John 56
Clark, John C. 10
Clark, Otis W.69
Clark,Patrick L.70
Clark, Thos. 23
Clark, Thos. 50
Clark, Wm. 41
Clark, Wm.G. 83
Clark, Wm.H. 76
Clark, Wm.H. 60
CLARKE, FRANCIS 3,45
Clarke, Thos.M. 73
CLARKE, WM.PHILO 14
Clarkins, John 6
Clayton, Thos. 90
Cleave, Robt. 91
Cleeland, Wm.J. 14
Clements,Bennett A.
         (Dr.) 54
Clements, John 80
Cleveland, Jas. 73
Cleveland,John E.29
CLIFFORD, WALTER 3,10
Cling, Samuel 20
Close, Lewis 43
Cloutier, Geo. 59
Clyde, Edward 34
Coakley,Patrick 38

C

Coakly, Patrick 9
Coble, Chas.T. 56
Cochran, David 77
Cochran,Orison C.13
Cochrane,John F. 83
Cody, Wm. F. 54
  ('Buffalo Bill')
Coffan, Edward 60
Coffey,Stephen J.48
Cogan, John 90
Cogan,Richard 50
Cogan, Wm. 68
Cohen, Geo.H.49
Colecroft, Wm.B.86
Cole, Ellis 58
Cole, Luther 41
Cole, John 48
Cole, Monroe 83
Coleman, Thos.W.30
Collins, Chas. 48
Collins,Cornelius
            43
Collins, Henry G.
          68,93
Collins, Jas. 8
Collins, Jas. 61
Collins, John 62
Collins, John E.71
Collins,Marvin 67
Collins,Mathew 90
Collins, Thos.12
Collins,Thos.F.52
Collins,Thos.K.15
Collins, Wm. 29
Collins, Wm.H.56
Coleman, Jas. 1
Colter,Richard P.
             83
Colwell,Warner 22
Comber, John B.78
Commoch,Frank 51
Comstock,Frank L.
              52
Conahan, Chas.63
Conboy, Thos. 87
Condon, David 60
Conelly,Patrick 36
Conklin,Ausburn B.
              14
Conklin, Jas. 84
Conklin, Wm.78
Conlan, Thos.32
Conley, John 79

Conlin, Edward 87
Conlin,Michael R. 84
Connell, John 30
Connell, Maurice 73
Connell, Michael 23
Connelly, Jas. 83
Conner, Andrew 29
Conner, John J. 8
Connerton, Thos.90
Conniff, Jas. 68
Conniff,Peter H. 13
Connolly, John 56
Connolly, Wm.M. 65
Connors, Michael 69
Conroy, Jas. 48
Considine, Thos. 65
Constantine, Chas.59
Conway, Jas. 76
Conway, Michael 72
Conway, Wm. 45
Cook, Edgar B. 39
Cook, Geo. 17
Cook, Herbert 31
Cook, John 72
Cook, Samuel 80
COOLIDGE, CHAS.A. 8
Coon, Holmes L. 6
Cooney, Gustav 34
Cooper, Geo. 41
Cooper, Wm.P.70,93
Copely, Robt. 11
Copestick, Wm. 23
Copley, Jos.W. 85
Corcoran, Daniel 22
Corcoran, John 31
Cordello, Wm. 37
Corley, Jos. 40
Corliss, Chas.P.68
Cornell, Jos.H. 33
Cornwall, Oscar 69,
            93
Corwin,Richard W.29
Cory,Jeremiah 69
Cosgriff, Jas. 68
Cosgrove, Thos. 54
Costello, Jas. 11
Coster, Robt. 68
Costigan, Jas. 23
Costigan, Wm. 18
Coulter, Wm. 68
Courtney,Edward M.
              78
Courtney,John A.67

Couzens, Thos. 43
Covert, John 53
Covery, Eli 48
Cowen, Robt.H. 14
Cowley,Cornelius 29
Cowley, Michael 14
Cowley, Stephen 26
Cox, John 17
Cox, Roddy 52
Cox, Thos. 32
Coy, Geo. 88
Coyle, Geo. 70
Coyle, Jos. 64
Craft, Louis 68
Craig, John 24
Craile, Wm.F. 33
Cramer, Thos. 77
Crans, Geo.W. 22
Crandall, Chas.A.31
CRAWFORD, EMMET 66,78
Crawford, Jacob W.21
Crawford,'Capt.Jack'
              54
Crawford,Richard M.42
Creamer,Bernard 91
Creighton,John C. 38
Creme, John 80
Cressey,Melancthon H.
              35
Creswell,Richard N.68
Cridland, John 62
Crimp, Wm.H. 62
Criswell, Benj.C. 30
Criswell, Geo.G. 73
Criswell, Henry 30
CRITTENDEN, ALBERT B.
            82,85
Crittenden, Harley 86
Crocker, Marshall 86
Croley, Wm.I. 70,93
Croley, Jas. 89
Cromley,Edward B. 37
Cronin, Michael 42
CROOK, GEORGE 54
Crosby, Wm.H. 19
Cross, Wm.'Billy' 2
Crouch, Edward 85
Crowe, Michael 30
Crowley,Michael 20
Crowley, Patrick N.18
Crowley, Patrick 30
Crump, John 30
Cryden, John 64

C

Cuddy, Martin 89
Culbertson,Ferdinand
          A. 29
Cullen, Bernard F.81
Cullen, Terence 92
Cullen, Wm. 85
Culligan, Thos. 1
Cullom, Geo.W. 8
Culpepper,Marcus 60
Cummins, John H.19
Cunliffe,Richard M.
          12
Cunnungham,Albert 32
Cunningham, Chas. 30
Cunningham,Frank  75
Cunningham,Michael
          84
Cunningham,Richard
          62
Cunningham, Wm. 56
Cunningham,Wm.J.68
Curley, Henry E.81
Curran, Thos. 11
Curry, Hugh 73
Curtis, John 19
Curtis, John 89
Curtis, Sam. J. 69
Curtiss, Wm.A. 34
Cushing, Thos. 51
Czaia, Albert 61

D

Dachend, Geo. 46
Dahl, John 57
Dahlman, Carl 83
Daily,Matthew 61
Daily,Patrick 53
Daily, Wm.H. 53
Dakna, Geo.H.52
Dale, Alfred W. 1
Dale, John 15
Dallam,Richard 57
Dalton, Wm. 59
Daly, Jas. 25
Daly, Jas. 91
Daly, John 51
Daly, Thos. 64
Dame, Marcus 91
Dammel,Gottlieb 90
Dangeleson,Otto 92
Daniel, August C.53
Daniels, Paul 8
Daniels, Zed H. 2

Dann, Geo. 32
Dannenfelsor,Henry 31
Darcey, John 64
Darcey, Jas. 69,93
Dark, Edward 46
Dark, John 18
Darney, John 46
Daum, Geo. 69
Davenport, Reuben 54
Davenport, Wm.H. 30
Davern, Edward 34
Davidson,Fernando 33
Davis, Albert 20
Davis, Chas.R. 17
Davis, Geo.W. 89
Davis, Harrison 40
Davis, John 33
Davis, John 68
Davis, John 73
Davis, John S. 76
Davis, John W. 17
Davis, Jos.H. 16
Davis,Lafayette 21
Davis, Richard 14
Davis,Richard L.58
Davis, Wm. 72
Davis, Wm. 85
Davis, Wm.N. 46
Dawsey, David E.32
Day, Chas.W. 68,93
Day, John 36
Day, Wm. H. 61
Day, Wm. L. 60
Dayton, Francis 39
Dean , Jas. P. 60
Dean, Wiley D. 15
Deats, Jack C. 85
DeCaskey, Fred. H.
          57
Decker,David H. 90
Decker, Peter 83
Deegan, Daniel 23
Deegan, Michael 86
DeHaven, Frank 75
Deily,Timothy 83
Deitline, Fred.32
Deitz, Leonard 19
Degnan, Bernard 83
Degner, Francis 50
DeGroot, Alfred 9
DeLacy, Milton 37
DeLany, Daniel 18

DELANEY, HAYDEN 82,86
Delaney, Jas. 87
Delaney, Michael 38
Delaney, Timothy 56
Deloney,Lawrence 70
Delmont, John 75
DeMott, Henry 69
Dempsey, John Q. 49
Dennis, Chas. 77
Dennis, Thos. 52
Denny, Sam. 51
Deprizin, Hugo 78
Deringer, Bernard 81
DERUDIO, CHAS. C.28,33
Derush, Jos. 92
Derwent, Jas.E. 62
Desmond, John 89
DeTourriel, Louis 30
Devereux,Phillip W.1,25
Devine, Jas. 83
Devine, John 59
Devlin, Jas. 83
Devlin, Neal 21
DeVoto,Augustus L.30
DEWEES, THOS. BULL 66,67
Dewey, Geo.W. 36
Dexter, Ruben P. 83
Diamond, Edward 36
DICKEY, CHAS. J. 3,41
Dickinsen, Thos J.67
Dickinson,Richard B.8
Dickson, Robt. 84
Diebert, Jas. B. 53
Diehl, Chas.S. 2
Diehr, Fred. 90
Dien, Wm. 41
Dignon, Jas. 19
Dillon, Chris. 86
Dillon, Francis 44
Dillon, Malachi 76
Dillon, Richard 76
Dinnsen, Amos 48
Dinsmore, Geo.W. 37
Dinsmore, Jas.M. 53
Dipp, Jas. R. 16
Dishner, John 53
Dixon, Geo. 37
Dixon, Jas. 45
Doan, Barnum 91
DOANE, GUSTAVUS C.15
Dodds, Nicholas 31
Doe, Wm. 39
Doherty, John F. 75

D

| | | |
|---|---|---|
| Doherty, Patrick 68 | Dowd, Morris 48 | Dusold, John 63 |
| Doherty, Thos. 62 | Dowden, Patrick 46 | Dustin, Wm. G. 50 |
| Dolan, John 40 | Dowling, David F.83 | Dwyer, Edmond 35 |
| Dolfer, Andrew 76 | Dowling,Patrick J.76 | Dwyer, Edward 49 |
| Doll,Jacob W.26 | Downey, John 72 | Dwyer, Patrick 87 |
| Dollmair,Weaver 70 | Doyale, Thos. 48 | Dyer, Robt. 68 |
| Domeck, Benj. 68 | Doyle, Francis 87 | Dyke, Peter 77 |
| Dommitt,Daniel 10 | Doyle, Jas. 6 | DYKMAN, WM. N. 43 |
| Donaghue,Patrick42 | Doyle, Wm. S. 25 | |
| Donahue, John 43 | Drager, Theodore 60 | E |
| Donahue,Michael T. 77 | Drake, Isaac S. 81 | |
| Donaldson,Uriah67 | Dreher, Karl 72 | Eades, Wm. 34 |
| Donavan, Dennis24 | Drew, Jas. 8 | Earls, Geo. W. 89 |
| Donlay, Jas. 56 | Drew, Daniel 42 | Easley, John T. 29 |
| Donley, Thos. 89 | Drummond,Samuel R. 44 | East, Henry B. 62 |
| Donnelly,Edward86 | Drusselmeir,John H. 24 | Eath, Jacob 91 |
| Donnelly,Michael H. 61 | Duane, John 10 | EATON, GEO. O. 56 |
| Donnelly, John 56 | Dubern, Frank 85 | Eberhardt,Rudolph 59 |
| Donnelly,John F.58 | Dubois, Wm.B. 74 | ECKERSON, EDWIN P.28, 34 |
| Donnelly,John S.51 | Duchman, Benj. 53 | Ecrestain, Wm. 87 |
| Donnelly,Stephen49 | Dudley, Wm. 69 | Eddy, Jas. M. 52 |
| Donahue, John 38 | Duffour,Abraham60 | Edele, Chris. 65 |
| Donahue, Wm. 40 | Duffy, Jas. 64 | Edeler, Wm. 52 |
| Doody, Wm. 87 | Duffy, Jas. 88 | Edgar, Geo. M. 78 |
| Dooley,Dennis 85 | Duffy, John 18 | EDGERLY, WINFIELD S. 28,32 |
| Dooley, Jas. 22 | Duffy, John 61 | Edwards, Chas.F.68,93 |
| Dooley,Patrick 64 | Duffy,Michael 60 | Edwards, John 83 |
| Doran, Miles 90 | Duffy, Owen P.20 | Edwards, Junius 90 |
| Dorn, August 75 | Duffy, Thos. 16 | Edwards, Paul 53 |
| Dorney, Jas. 46 | Dugan, Jas. 51 | Edwards,Spencer 18 |
| Dorsey,Martin 53 | Dugan, John 15 | Edwards, Wm. 52 |
| Dougherty, Chas.75 | Dugan, Lawrence84 | Edwards, Wm.H. 80 |
| Dougherty, Jas. 30 | Duggan,Andrew P.61 | Efferts,Matthias 10 |
| Dougherty,Jas.B.41 | Duggan,Dennis B.81 | Egan, Eugene 33 |
| Dougherty,Michael 61 | Duggan,John E.14 | Egan, John G. 52 |
| Dougherty,Michael 86 | Dunivan, Thos.87 | Egert, Chas. 17 |
| Dougherty,Wm.J.70, 93 | Dunlap, John 25 | Ehred, Jacob J. 91 |
| Doughty,Thos.J.59 | Dunn, Richard 44 | Ehrig,Wentelin 74 |
| Doughty,Wm.F. 68 | Dunn,Timothy J.42 | Eichweitzel,Chas.F.76 |
| Douglas, Geo.E.70 | Dunn, Thos. 34 | Einbaum,Lewis G. 6 |
| Douglas, Jas. 42 | Dunnigan, Jos. 91 | Eisenberg,John C.86 |
| Douglas, Wm. 63 | Dunnigan,Patrick52 | Eisenberger,Peter 26 |
| Douglass,John E.81 | Durand, Emile 45 | Elsenheimer,Bernard83 |
| Douglass,Milton F. 70 | Duren,Orlando H.76 | Eiskamp, Louis 83 |
| Dow, Frank E. 39 | Durkin, John 67 | Elden, Perry A.74 |
| Dowd, Chas. O.52 | Durning,Osborne C. 45 | Elder, John W. 75 |
| | Durrslew,Earnest 42 | Elgie, Wm.J. 44 |
| | Durslen, Otto 29 | Elkins, John R. 16 |
| | | Elliott, Robt. V. 57 |
| | | Ellis, Jas. 67 |

E

Ellis, Wm. A. 21
Ellison, Frank 31
Elrich,Jerome A. 92
Elward, Chas. 86
Elwell, Chas. 44
Elwood, Stephen 37
Emerich, Jacob 26
Emerson, Edward 92
Emery, Jas. B. 45
Emmet, Robt. 77
Emmons, Chas. 71
Emory, Geo. 57
Engel, Franz 51
Engelhardt,Peter 18
Englehorn, Wm.T. 70
English, Fred.P. 78
ENGLISH, WM. L.3,12
Enos, David 65
Enright, Thos. 24
Eraus, Wm.W. 57
Erb, Julius 65
Erhard, Frank V.81
Eshelman,David N.88
Estabrook,Frank W.77
Etzler, Wm. 39
Eubin, Jos. 64
EVANS, ANDREW W. 66
Evans, Fred. W. 69
Evans, Herbert O. 6
Evans, Wm. 10
Exford, Gilbert 81

F

Fagan, John 59
Fairbanks (courier)
                54
Falardo, John 18
Fallon, Patrick 12
Fannin, Chas.W. 6
Farmer, Jess H. 86
Farnham, Frank 89
Farrel, Martin 43
Farrell, Jas. 14
Farrell, Jos.L. 7
Farrell,Michael 49
Farrell, Thos. 18
Farrer, Morris 31
Farrington,Francis
             H. 49
Fassold, Lewis 89
Faulman, Wm. 87

Fay, John J. 32
Feaha, Wm. W. 22
Featherall, Wm.72
Featherly, Wm. 77
Fehler, Henry 29
Feighery, John 60
Feil, Herman 92
Felber, Edward 25
Fellhart, Samuel 63
Felmacher, Emil 45
Felt,Sumner B. 48
Fennel, Anthony 62
Fenton, Isaac H.60
Ferguson. Byron D.
                78
Ferguson,Edward M.
                11
Ferguson, Jas. 84
Ferguson, Thos. 76
Ferguson, Wm.75
Fergusson,Franklin
                61
Ferrers, Geo. 20
Ferster, Henry 78
Field, Gerard K.52
Fillery, Daniel 63
Fillman, Oliver 60
Finch, Wm.H. 72
Finerty, John F.54,
                93
Finigan,Patrick J.
                11
Finnegan, Henry 56
Finnegan,Thos.J.34
Fischer, Chas. 40
Fisher, Alvis 43
Fisher, Frank 49
Fisher, Geo. 71
Fisher, Robt. 75
Fisk, Chas.L. 80
Fitzgerald,Michael
                72
Fitzgerald,John 15
Fitzgerald,John 26
Fitzgerald,John 56
Fitzimmens,Michael
                46
Fitzimmons,Patrick
                18
Fitzpatrick,Andrew
                45
Fitzpatrick,Michael
          J. 73

Fitzpatrick,Owen 85
Fitzpatrick,Sylvester
                24
Fitzsimons,John F.49
Flanagan,Barney 86
Flanagan,Dennis 46
Flanagan, Jas. 32
Flanigan, Joel S. 16
Flanigan, John 17
Flannery, Thos. 75
Flatley, Francis 58
Fleming, Jos. 65
Fleming, Julius B.18
Flemming, John 69
Flemming,Oliver G.60
Flemming, Thos. 57
Flint, Robt. 75
Flohn, Jacob 91
Flood, Edward, Jr. 79
Flood, Mathew 90
Flood, Patrick 75
Flood,Phillip A. 62
Flood, Thos. 73
Flynn, Aloah 41
Flynn,Bartholemew 50
Flynn, Richard 83
Foerstall, Geo. 33
Fogarty, Michael 13
Folckman, Wm. 59
Foley, Jeremiah 76
Foley, John 38
Foley, John 76
Foley, Jos. 58
Foley, Maurice 60
Foley, Michael 22
Fonss,Fred.W.S. 78
FORBES, THEODORE Y.47,51
Forborg, Chas. H. 89
FORBUSH, WM. C. 55
Ford, Augustus W. 9
Ford, Daniel 61
Ford, Geo. J. 49
Ford, Wm. 85
Foreaker, Jas.P. 23
Forristel, Jas. 69
Forster, Frank 70
Fortson, Conrad 56
Fosbenner,Albert D. 60
Foss, Frank W. 71
Foster, Aaron B. 91
Foster, Chas. 73
Foster, Geo. 81

F

FOSTER, JAS.E.H.66
                    79
Foster, John A. 81
Foster, Henry 85
Foster, Peter 79
Foulk, Geo. 1
Fowler, Isaac 31
Fowler,Richard 19
Fox, Adam 68
Fox, Chas. 19
Fox, Francis 58
Fox, Harvey A.32
Fox, Jas. 57
Fox, John 32
Fox, Jos. 23
Fox, Patrick 50
France, Fred. 67
Francis, John 60
Frank, John 52
Frank, John F.24
Frank. Wm. 30
Franklin,John W.29
Franklin,Mills 39
Fraser, John 49
Frazier, Geo. 62
Frederick,Andrew38
FREEMAN, HENRY B.
            3,11
Freeman,Patrick 78
Freiberg,Augustus
                    11
FRENCH,THOS.H.4,
        28,40
Frew, Jas. B.59
Friegel, John 68
Frink, Alvah C.49
Frisby, Wm. 84
Fritz, Henry R.88
Fritz, Jacob 56
Fritz; Lewis 56
Frost,Peter W.6
Frost, Thos.12
Fry, John 77
Fry, Wm. 57
Fryling, Wm. 69
Fulk, Henry 61
Fuller, Henry E.
                    61
Fullmer, Jacob49
Fulton, Alex. 59
Funk,Alfred F.83
Funk, Wm. 10
FUREY, JOHN V.54

Furman,Howard G. 89
Fussel, Fred. G. 65
Fussner, John J. 92
Futterer, John 58

G

Gable, Wesley 68
Gabriel, Daniel 70
Gafferly, Edward 60
Gaffney, Geo. 37
Gaghagan,Ambrose 90
Gahlsdorf, Fred. 78
Gallagher, Daniel 17
Gallagher, Francis65
Gallagher, Francis90
Gallagher, John 71
Gallagher, John 84
Gallagher, Jos. 13
Gallagher, Jos. 73
Gallenne,Jean B.D.40
Galvin, Jas. 73
Gandley, Jas. 78
Gannon, Peter 30
Gardiner, Chas.J.65
Gardner, Chas.H. 60
Gardner, Robt. 88
GARLINGTON,ERNEST A.
        4,28.35
Garlock,Walter E.13
Garnier, Baptiste 54
  ("Little Bat")
GARRETTY,FRANK D. 19
Garvey, Francis 59
Gaskill, Jas. 87
Gates, John 31
Gatz, Philip H. 88
Gau, Walter 74
Gauruauard (sp.)
        John B. 91
Gavin, Anthony 43
Gayle, Wm.G. 23
Geaged (sp.),Jos.H.
                    44
Gearsley, Jonas 45
Geesbacher,Gabriel
                    37
Gehrmann, Fred.H.30
Geiger, Frank 9
Geiger, Geo. 36
Geist, Frank 35
Genand, Jas. 50
Gentles, Wm. 91

Gentzer, Frank 90
George, Philip 83
Gerhardt, Chas. 59
Gerster, Jacques 43
Gesell, Geo. 85
Ghortill, Thos. 60
GIBBON, JOHN 3,5
Gibbons, Patrick M.92
Gibbs, Chas. S. 50
GIBBS, EUGENE B. 2
Gibbs, Jas. G. 59
Gibbs, Wm. 38
Gibbs, Winfield S.65
Gibney, Thos. 25
GIBSON,FRANCIS M.4,28,
                .35,36
Gibson, Jas. 65
Gibson, Jos. 53
Gibson, Samuel 86
Gilbert, Chas.M. 59
Gilbert, John M. 29
Gilbert, Louis 70
Giles, Dennis 77
Gilligan,Michael T.61
Gilman, Edward 59
Gilmore, Thos.B. 16
Giltman,Michael 50
Glackewsky, Frank 14
Glancey, John 70
Glannon,Michael 76
Glanon, Thos. 78
Glasheen, Edward 77
Glass, Edward 76
Glass, Samuel A. 17
Glasure, Eugene H. 68
Glawinski, Albert 81
Glease, Geo.W. 36
  (real name: Glenn,G.W.)
Glenn, Wm. 46
Glenn, Wm.H. 59
Glick, Wm. E. 87
Glock, Henry 67
Glover, Thos.B. 68
Glucing,Heinrich 74
Glynn, Jas. 58
Goddard,Marcellus 80
GODFREY, EDWARD S. 4,
                28,38
Godfrey, Samuel 84
Goff, Chas. 34
Goggin, John 37
Goldberg, Jacob 13
Golden, Bernard 40

G

Golden, Jas. 72
Goldin, Theo.W. 35
Goldsmith, John 65
Gomely, Jas. 21
Goodenough,Andrew J.
                41
GOODLOE,ARCHIBALD 3,
                42
Goodwin, Jas. E. 7
Gordon, Chas. 72
Gordon, Jas. 21
Gordon, Thos.A. 38
Gorman, Jas. 50
Goslin, _____ 1
Goss, Jas. 90
Gould, Thos. 43
Goyer, Edwin 39
Graemer,Michael 68
Grady, Edmund 68
Graham, Alex. 68
Graham, Chas.E.42
Graham, Chas.G.71
Graham, John 63
Graham, Thos.14
Graham, Thos.35
Graham, Thos.W.19
Grammer, Wm.H. 44
Granberry, Geo.L.64
Granberry, Thos.W.86
Granger, Geo. 52
Grannickstadten,
        John 68
Grant, Eugene 11
Grant, Thos. 60
Granville,Edward G.
                14
Grappenstetter,
    Mathew 81
Graves, 'Capt.' 54
Gray, Henry E. 16
Gray, Henry W. 12
Gray, John 30
Gray, Wm.S. 35
Grayson, Edward 35
Grazierni,Lawrence L.
                72
Greancy, Geo. 64
Green, Edwin A. 58
Green, Fulton 31
Green, Hugh 67,93
Green, John N. 74
Green, Jos. 32

Green, Thos. 38
Green, Wm. 84
Greenbauer, Geo. 67
Greene, John A. 45
Greene,Martin V. 65
Greenwald, Jos. 19
Gregg,Richard G. 85
Gregg, Wm.J. 34
Greuther, August 45
Grey, John 64
Griesner, Julius 26
Griffin, Edwin M.72
Griffin, Thos. 49
Griffith, Jas. 58
Griffith, Wm. 80
Grigsby, Lewis S.76
Grillon, Chas. 16
Grimes, R.B. 54
Groff, Henry S. 7
Grosh, Andrew 79
Groshan, Fred. 9
Gross, John 77
Grouard, Frank54,93
Gruel, Wm. 42
Gruver, Jas. 19
Guetzey, Herman 44
Guinnan, John 60
Gundera, Frank 51
Gunker, August 84
Gunn,Augustus S. 65
Gunther, Chas. 39
Gutike, Paul 68
Guy, Zachery Y. 87
Gynau, Thos. 72


H

Haack, Henry 36
Haakinson, Maught57
Habergarten, Adam50
Hackett, John 35
Hackett, Thos. 77
Haddo, John 48
Haddock, Chas. 58
Hagdorn, Wendel 92
Hagenbach, Fred.37
Hagerty,Luther C.88
Hale, Henry H. 62
Hale, John 78
Haley, John 63
Haley, Timothy 36
Hall,_____ 1

Hall, Chas. E. 14
Hall, Curtis 32
Hall, Elijah 11
Hall, John 57
Hall, John G. 71
Hall, John W. 90
Hall, Wm. A. 22
HALL, WILLIAM P. 55
Halverson, Ole 23
Halvey, Thos. 62
Hamill, Frank 86
Hamilton, Andrew 29
Hamilton,Edward J.6
Hamilton, Edwin 78
Hamilton, Geo. 53
Hamilton, Henry 22
Hamilton, John 59
Hamilton,Michael 50
HAMILTON, SAMUEL T.
                4,17
Hammer, Chas. 44
Hammer, Geo. 72
Hammon, John E. 35
Hampford, Ford 61
Hanernas, Geo. 76
Hanley , Patrick 89
Hanley,Richard P.31
Hanlin, John 52
Hanne, Henrick 43
Hannold, Robt. 46
Hansel, Albert 51
Hansen, Chas.P. 78
Hansen, Marcus 76
Hanshammer, Fred. 86
Hanson, Edward B. 22
Happi, Julius 86
Hardden, Wm. 32
Hardin, Wm. R. 87
Hardy, John 1
Hardy, Wm.G. 2,29
HARE, LUTHER R.28,39
HARGOUS, CHAS. F.47,52
Harker, Alex. 59
Harlfinger, Gustav 26
Harlin, John 49
Harmon, John 50
Harney, Richard 83
Harper,Emerson G. 58
Harrigan, Daniel 80
Harrington, Edward 14
Harrington,Gregory P.
                67,93

H

Harrington, John 61
Harrington, Jos.E.65
Harrington, Thos 8
Harris, David W. 29
Harris, Geo. 74
Harris, Henry 45
Harris, Jas. 32
Harris, John 60
Harris, John H. 59
Harris, Wm. 19
Harris, Wm. 48
Harris, Wm.M. 32
Harrison, Henry 59
Harrison, Jos. 59
Harrison, Thos.W.32
Hart, Chas.J. 42
Hart, Francis 68
Hart, Osker C. 64
Hart, Silas 39
Hart, Wm. 74
HARTSUFF, ALBERT(Dr.)
                    54
Harvey, Jas. 63
Harvey, P.H.(Dr.) 2
Hasson,Patrick68,93
Hasting, Wm. 56
Hastings,Frank E.9
Hastings,Maurice 72
Hatchcock,Frank W.79
Hatcher, Chas.J. 52
HATHAWAY,FORREST H.
                    47
Hathaway, Geo. 44
Hattier, Earnest 60
Hawkins, Samuel S.89
Hawks, Morgan B. 76
Hay, Samuel 61
Hayer, John 32
HAYES, EDWARD M.55,
                    62
Hayes, Henry 89
Hayes, Jas. 67
Hazeltine,David R.43
Heald, Benj. 79
Healey, John 84
Healey,Michael 87
Healy, John 65
Hearn, Thos. 56
Hearst, Geo. 60
Heaslip, Irving 83
Heath, Robt.W. 60
Heaton, David 7

Hecht, Carl 69
Hecker, John 77
Hedley,Joseph B.58
Hefferman,Daniel C.
                    33
Hegancy, Patrick48
Hegner, Francis 34
Heid, Geo. 40
Heider, Levi 8
Heinbaugh, John 49
Heinemann, Geo.64
Heinze, Chas. 6
Heinzman, Adolph 8
Heinzmann,Jos. 48
Heird, Jacob70,93
Hekel, Jacob 78
Helmbold,Alfred74
Helzer,August J.84
Helvia, Wm.E. 84
Henden, David 89
Henderson,Geo.K.26
Henderson, Rufus21
Hendricksen,Thad.N.
                    88
Hendrickson, Sam.
                    17
Henery,Harvey 87
Hennessey,Patrick
                    76
Henning,Chas.M. 49
Henry,Albert J. 62
Henry, Edward 65
Henry,Fritz H. 78
Henry,Isaac B. 43
Henry, Jas.P. 67
Henry, John 79
Henry,Robt. Fitz
                    88
Hensley, Wm. 10
Herald, Henry 76
Herbert, Julius91
Herd, Wm. 74
Herendeen. Geo. 2
Herhold, Herman68
Herlihy,Michael 52
Herr, John C. 37
Herrins, Benj. 46
Hershler, Fred. 77
Hetler, Jacob 32
Heuser, Jos. 19
Hewitt, Jas. 20
Heynemann,Henri 69

Hickey, Albert 52
Hickia, Patrick 64
Hickman, Wm.F. 60
Hicks, Chas. 58
Hiet, John 62
Higbee, John R. 62
Higerty, Patrick 83
Higgson, John 62
Hike, Andrew 53
Hill, Chas.R. 11
Hill, Frank E. 60
Hill, Jas. 30
Hill, John T. 92
Hill, Harry B. 34
Hill, Thos. 80
Hill, Wm. G. 76
Hills, Wm. A.68,93
Hincer, Harrison 80
Hiners, Henry 65
Hines, Chas.H. 79
Hines, Lewis 13
Hinkle, Andrew J. 48
HINKLE, FRANK S. 50
Hinkler, Wm. 9
Hinkley,Merritt E.41
Hinternesch,Henry 89
Hinton, Thos. 15
Hinze, Robt.H. 72
Hiram, Thos.W. 87
Hird, John B. 31
Hirschberg,Solomon 86
Hivaley, Otis W. 90
Hoady, John 61
Hoalt, John 48
Hobbs, John W. 73
Hobsen, Jos.N. 74
Hocksmith,August 87
Hod, Chas. 53
Hoehn, Max 27
Hoffman,Emanuel L.22
Hoffman, John 63
Hoffman, John 70
Hoffman,Lummen W. 7
Hoffstetter, Geo. 76
Hogan, John 49
Hogan, Henry 51
Hogan, Michael 12
Hogeboom,Peter L.81
Hogg, David 70
Hogland, Alonzo 78
Hohman,Leopold 49
Holahan, Andrew 38

H

Holden, Jas. 92
Holden, Henry 32
Holkins,Gottlieb 50
Holland, Chas.H.31
Holledered,Geo.79
Hollen, Peter 76
Hollenbecker,John
                70
Holley, Louis 53
Holpe, Anton 34
Holtz, Jos. 87
Hone,Samuel W.69,
         93
Honicker,Francis 10
Hood, Chas. W. 36
Hood, Samuel 59
Hook, Stanton 29
HOOTEN, MOTT 3,46
Hoover,Thos. S. 16
Hopkins, Samuel C.
                44
Hoppe, Wm. 31
Horgan, Dan 51
Horn, Geo. 32
Hornaday,Simpson61
Horner, Jacob 27
Hornick, Jos. 89
Horton, Jos. 89
Hose, Geo. 38
Houghtaling,Chas.H.
                32
Houts, John C. 65
Howard, Angelo 23
Howard, Frank 34
Howard, Geo. 23
Howard, Geo.C.58
Howard, Geo.G.11
Howard, Geo.L.70
Howard, Jas.Wm. 2
  ('Phocion')
Howard, John 10
Howard, John 68
Howard, Henry 23
Howe, Jos. 80
Hoyt, Walter 27
Hoyt, Wm. 52
Hubbard,Lewis G.10
Hubert, John 79
Hucksmith,August87
Hudson, Wm.K. 89
Huebner, Chas. 33
Huff, Jacob 42
Hug, Alois 52

Hughes, Frank 23
Hughes, Jas. 49
Hughes, John 48
HUGHES, ROBT. P. 2
Hughes, Thos. 36
Hughes, Thos. 86
Hugler,Ferdinand 43
Hulohan, Thos. 92
Humfress, Louis 43
Humme,Paul F.A. 55
Hummell, Albert 23
Hunselkuse,John 53
Hunt, Chas. A. 52
Hunt, Edward 52
Hunt,Frederick O.48
Hunt, Geo. 32
Hunt, John 36
Hunt, Samuel 86
Hunter, Frank 34
Hunter, Geo.A. 60
Hunter, John 19
HUNTER, WM. C.55,56
Huntington, Alex.68
Huntington,Chas.P.
                65
HUNTINGTON, HENRY D.
              66,69
Hupman, Jacob C. 50
Hurd, Jas. 32
Hurlburt, Philo O.
                13
Hurley, Thos. 50
Hurt, Jas.M. 79
Hutchinson,Geo.W.75
Hutchinson,Rufus D.
                30
Hutchison,John M.53
Huth,Morris H. 15
Hyland,Michael 44
Hynds, Hugh 21
Hyner, Wm. 42


I

Ickler, Wm. 9
Igglesden, Jos. 6
Imsauda, Henry 64
Irving, John 15
Isaac, Eugene 69
Isgrigg, Robt. M. 7

J

Jabowing, Geo. 9
Jackson, John 69
Jackson, Robt. 2
Jackson, Wm.'Billy' 2
Jacob, Samuel 86
Jacobs,Abraham 69
Jacobs, Jos. 22
JACOBS, JOSHUA WEST 5
Jaeger, Chas.W. 42
James, Nicholas 6
Jamison, Wm. 43
Jansen, Julius 77
Jansen, Peter 76
Jarvis, Albert 57
Jarvis, Geo. 57
Jeffers, Jas. 59
Jefferson,Henry W.60
Jenkins, Miles W. 60
Jenkins, Wm. 17
Jennys, Alonzo 38
Jensen, Neil C. 63
Jephson,Frederick 50
Jester,Leander R.31
Joergeus, John H. 64
JOHNSON, ALFRED B. 12
Johnson, Andrew 86
Johnson, Chas. 24
Johnson, Chas. 61
Johnson, Chris. 58
Johnson, Francis 37
Johnson, Henry 74
Johnson, Jas. 51
Johnson, John 1
Johnson, John 56
Johnson, Peter 49
Johnson, Robt. 39
Johnson, Robt. 71
Johnson, Samuel 29
Johnson,Theodore L.87
Johnson, Wm. 74
Johnston, Benj. 35
Johnston, Jas. 92
Johnston, Wm. 84
Jolly, Jas. 53
Jones, Albert H. 11
Jones, Chas. F. 68
Jones, Eugene 75
Jones, Griffith 24
Jones, Henry P. 37
Jones, Jas. M. 39
Jones, John R. 62
Jones, John W. 14
Jones, Peter 33

J

Jones, Robt.F. 18
Jones, Thos. 14
Jones, Thos. 90
Jones,Washington 69
Jones, Wm.H. 17
Jonsen, Peter 76
Jonson, Emil O. 29
Joosteen,John L.69
Jordan, Henry 37
Jordan, John 31
Jordan, John J. 90
Jordan, John W. 77
Jordan, Wm. W. 90
Joslin, Snoch A.52
Jourdain,Francois73
Joyce, Matthew 34
Juergeus,John H. 64
Jungsbluth,Julius26
Just , Chas. 44

K

Kaapp,Samuel S. 39
Kade,Fred. 60
Kail, John 83
Kaiser,Christie 14
Kalber, Adolph 78
Kales, Geo.W. 57
Kamer, Louis 25
Kamphouse,Barney18
Kane, Geo.F. 16
Kane,Patrick 51
Kane,Patrick 84
Kane, Wm. 26
Kane, Wm.J. 53
Karche, John 91
Kash, Theodore61
Katzenmaier,Jacob35
Kaufman, Geo.D. 72
Kaufman, Henry 62
Kavanagh, Jas. 32
Kavannagh, Chas.40
Kearney,John 75
Kearney,Michael 15
Kearns, John 52
Keating, Chas. 13
Keating,Patrick 49
Kee, Henry 69
Keefe, Jas. 62
Keefe, John J. 26
Keegan, Chas.J.12
Keegan, John 6

Keegan,Michael 27
Keegan, Thos. 42
Keegan, Thos. 48
Keeks, John 53
Keeland, Edward 73
Keeler, Henry 20
Keenan, Chas. 90
Keenan, Jas. 69
Keenright,Walter B.
                    71
Keife, Barney 87
Keith, Geo. 58
Keith, John 56
Keith, John J. 43
Kelch, Frank 42
KELL, WILLIAM H.46
Keller, John 32
Kellerman, Geo. 20
Kelley, John 67
Kelliher, Paul 92
KELLOGG, SANFORD C.
                 55,63
Kelly, Bernard 76
Kelly, Edward 91
Kelly, Geo. 36
Kelly, Jas. 19
Kelly, Jas. 30
Kelly, Jas. 36
Kelly, Jas. 64
Kelly, Jas. 75
Kelly, John 43
Kelly, John P.59
Kelly, Luther 2
('Yellowstone')
Kelly, Mathew 49
Kelly,Michael 17
Kelly,Patrick 42
Kelly,Patrick 48
Kelly,Patrick 76
Kelly,Patrick 92
Kelly, Thos. 16
Kelly, Thos. 52
Kelly, Thos. 68
Kelly, Wm. 21
Kelly, _____ 54
Kelson, John C.62
Kelton, Isaac J.81
Kempe, Wm.B. 57
KENDRICK, FRED.M.H.
                    11
Kenecht, John 56
Kennedy,Andrew 16

Kennedy, Edward 58
Kennedy,Jackson 6
Kennedy, Jas. 46
Kennedy,Lawrence 72
Kennedy, Wm.B. 89
KENNINGTON, JAS.82,89
Kenny, John 22
Kent, Wm. 84
Kern, John 16
Kernan, Hugh 18
Kerwin, Philip 61
Kessel, John 39
Kett, Henry 77
KEYES, EDWARD L.55,58
Kevery, John H. 75
Kieley,Jeremiah 22
Kifer, Albert 7
Kilfoyle, Martin 26
Killiganey,Richard 57
Kimball, J.P.(Dr.) 2
Kimber, Clarence 34
Kimm, John G. 33
Kinder, Herman J. 72
KING, ALBERT D.66,73,79
KING, CHAS. 55
King, Chas. 67
King, Frank 89
King, Geo. 33
King, Hervey 63
King, John 53
KINGSBURY, FRED.WM.66,71
Kingsley, Wm.C. 70
Kingston, Dick C. 79
KINZIE, FRANK X. 21
Kipp, Fremont 32
Kirby, Jas. 44
Kirby, Jos. 73
Kirby, Thos. 78
Kirkbride, Geo. 48
Kirkwood, John A. 81
Kirkwood, Wm. 71
KIRTLAND, THADDEUS S.3,9
Kistler, John 18
Klaweitter,Ferdinand 30
Klein, Chas. 45
Klein, Daniel 65
Klein, Frederick 87
Kleis, John 13
Klewitz, Jos. 6
Klingensmith, Samuel 61
Knapp, Howard 70
Knapp, Wm. 48

K

Knapper, Henry 71
Knaur, Wm.F. 52
Knight, Thos. 91
Knipe, Daniel 31
Knittell, Jacob 75
Knox, Jas. 9
Knox, John 75
Knowles, Chas.C.57
Knupper, Ferdinand
                    67
Koch, Jacob 85
Koch, Martin 57
Koekler, Gustave 56
Kogan, John F. 64
Kohlepp, Carl 19
Kohler, Eggert 68
Kohn, John 77
Kolaugh, Chas. 72
Kolby, Geo. 91
Kopp, Fred. 42
Korn, Gustav 37
Korslager,Barney63
Krager, Geo. 51
Kramer,Bernhard 85
Kramer, John 73
Krause, Alonzo 51
Kreasch, Geo.F. 43
Kreiger, Mathew 61
Kreissig, Geo. 86
Kremer, John 80
Krentz, John 53
Kretchmer, John 32
Kroll, Jos. 15
Kron, Chas.A. 37
Krone, Jas.L. 85
Kruger, Martin 19
Kuehl, Jesse 32
Kusbaum,Calvin 85
Kussman, Emil 61


L

Labegan, Geo. 51
Ladd, John 49
Laden, Jos. 35
Laffan, Dennis 59
Laffelbein,Rudolph
                    67
LaFine, Fred. 87
Laguer, Nichan (sp)
                    57
Lanigan,Michael F.
                    74

LaLande, Frank 88
Lalor, Wm. 40
LaMaire, John 45
Lamandon,Henry A.57
Lammers,Gerhard 44
Lamprey,Samuel B.62
Land, Wm. 70
Lane, Daniel 59
Lane, Riley R. 10
Lang, Edwin F. 41
Lang, Wm. 69
Langan, John 76
Lange, August 88
Lange, Henry 33
Langley,Danford R.
                    88
Langman, Anselm 79
Langton, Wm. 18
Langton, Wm. 62
Lanigan,Michael F.
                    74
Lannen, John 77
Laparr, John 37
LaPiene, Alfred 44
Larkin,Dennis W.81
Larkingland,Wm. 74
Larson, Chris. A.63
Larson, Chris. 84
Lasley, Wm.W. 38
Latham, Chas. 52
Lathrop,Barbour 54
Lattman, John 35
Lauper, Frank 35
Lauthammer,Chas.A.
                    14
Lavelle, Edward 76
Lavelle, Philip 45
Laverty, Jos. 69
Law, Thos. 53
Lawhorn, Thos. 36
Lawler, Jas. 31
Lawler, Jerome 57
Lawlor, Geo.T. 16
Lawrence, Leon 83
Lawson, Chas.F.23
LAWSON, JOS.66,72
Lawton, John J.59
Leak, John D. 74
Leary, Dennis 52
Leary, John 58
Leary, Wm. 79
Leber, Fred. 41

LeCompte, Wm. C. 54
Lee, Andrew 73
Lee, John 58
Lee, John C. 87
Lee, Wm. 73
Leech, Thos. 90
Lefler, Meig 34
LeForge, Thos. 2
Leggatt,Geo.E. 88
Leher, Geo. 8
Leher, Jas.C. 8
Lehman, Fred 74
Lehn, August 83
LEIB, EDWARD H.55,65
Leighton,Theodore P.68
Leills, Carl 63
Leipler, Wm. 14
Leitelt, Edward C.78
Leitz, Christian 15
LEMLY, HENRY R. 66
Lempke, John 44
Lenihan, Jas. 64
Leonard, Henry 72
Leonard, John 24
Leonard, Stephen 92
Leonard, Wm. S. 58
Lepper, Frederick 39
Leroy, Arthur 74
Leslie, Chas. 14
LEUTTWITZ, ADOLPHUS H.
          von 66,74,76
LeValley, Francis 59
Leverett, Cecil R. 38
Levett, Jos. W. 50
Lewis, Edward 67
Lewis, Fred. W. 55
Lewis, Geo. 91
Lewis, Isaac B. 65
Lewis, Jacob 46
Lewis, John 69
Lewis, Uriah S. 26
Lewis, Wm.C.C. 76
Liddle, Geo. H. 71
Liechty, Noah 49
Liel, Chas. 92
Lies, Henry 92
Lindenberg, Chas.H. 81
Lindsay, David 77
Lindsay, John D. 75
Linehau, Edward 12
Links, David 61
Lipthar,Augustus 90

L

Lister, Jos. 83
Litchfield,Oscar W.
                 24
Littlefield,John L.
                 26
Littlejohn,Amos W.
                 25
Livingston,Robt. 77
LLOYD, CHAS. F.82,89
Lloyd, Thos. 76
LOCKWOOD, BENJ. C.43
Loftus,Michael 52
Logan, Alfred 70
LOGAN, WILLIAM 3,8
Logue, Wm. 39
Lonagan, John 90
Lonargan,Patrick84
LONDON, ROBT.55,59,
                 63
Long, Francis 15
Long, Gilbert 83
Long, Jos. F. 70
Longrigg, John 73
Longstaff, Robt.61
Lookstedt,Walter 15
Loomis,Henry T. 52
Loomis,Reginald A.
                 73
Lorden,Dennis B.58
Lorentzen,Peter 11
Losciborski,John79
Louder, John H. 72
Louett, Wm. 12
Lough, Geo. 41
Louis, Frank 90
Louis, Fred. 58
Louissant,        54
Love, Geo.H. 24
Loving, Francis 56
Low, Philip 6
Lowden, Samuel 42
Lowe, Theodore 80
LOWE, WM. H.,Jr 4,
                 21
Lowee, Geo. F. 58
Lowell, Edward 21
Lowell, Henry 61
Lowell, Homer 48
Lown, Jas. 75
Lowrie, Alex. M.
                 87
Lowry, Geo. P.74
Lowry, Geo. W.79

Loyd, Geo. 35
LUHN, GERHARD L.82,
                 84
Lumior, Jas. F. 56
Lupton, Allen 76
Lurnbreger, Geo.L.
                 91
Lyman, Wm. H. 68
Lynch, Dennis 34
Lynch, Dennis 92
Lynch, Fred.H.57
Lynch, Henry 43
Lynch, John 72
Lynch,Patrick 37
Lynch,Patrick 77
Lynch,Richard 77
Lynch, Thos. 59
Lynch, Thos. 67
Lyons, Bernard 34
Lyons, Daniel 38
Lyons, Jas. 88
Lyons, John 20
Lyons, John 59
Lyons, Martin 42


M

Mack, Jacob 69
MACKLIN, JAS. C.45
MacIntosh, Wm. 7
MacKenzie, Frank69
MacKinnon, Chas.43
McAdams, Ernest L.
                 92
MCADAMS, JAS. G.16
McAleer,Patrick 91
McAllister,Andrew
                 37
McAlvey, Geo. 19
McAnulty, Geo.W.86
MCARTHUR, MALCOLM
                 19
McAtee, Wm. 51
McBlain, John F.17
McCabe, John 16
McCabe, John 30
McCabe, Thos. 59
McCaffery,Michael
                 15
McCall, John 46
McCandless,Wm.P.74
McCann,Bernard 42
McCann, John 72

McCann, John 88
McCarthy, Daniel 34
McCarthy, Edward B.2y
McCarthy, Frank 87
McCarthy, John 20
McCarthy,Michael 18
McCarthy,Patrick F. 18
McCarthy, Timothy 81
McCarty, John 84
McCauley, Wm. 45
McChesney, Jas. 78
McClain, John 78
McClanahan, Jos. 91
McCleery, Daniel 68
MCCLERNAND, EDWARD J.5,15
McClinton, Wm.J. 74
McCloskey, Edward 78
McClure, John 56
McClurg, Wm. 29
McCollum, Frank 6
McConnell, Frank 78
McConnell, John 57
McConnell, Hugh 73
McConnell, Wilson 38
McCook, Henry A. 67
McCoran, Patrick 56
McCormack, Daniel 83
McCormack, John 69
McCormick, Jas. 27
McCormick, John 21
McCormick, John 48
McCormick, John 88
McCormick, Michael 51
McCormick,Montgomery 70
McCormick, Samuel 35
McCormick, Thos. 64
McCougow,Richard H.45
McCoy, Charley 48
McCreedy, Thos. 31
McCue, Martin 38
McCue, Thos. 70
McCurdy, Ellis 63
McCurry, Jos. 36
McDermott, Geo.M. 29
McDermott, John 64
McDermott, Thos. 36
McDonald, Donald 63
McDonald, Edward 21
McDonald, Edward C. 62
McDonald, Geo. H. 80
McDonald, Hugh 44
McDonald, Jas. H. 65
McDonald, John 75

M

McDonald, John 57
McDonald, Thos. 16
McDonald, Wm. 74
McDonnell, John 35
McDonnell, Patrick 32
MCDOUGALL, THOS. M.
        4,28,30
McDuff, Jas. 67
McDunough, Jas. 35
McEagan, John 35
McElevey, Jos. 22
McElroy, Jas. 19
McElroy, Henry 57
McEnery, Patrick 84
McEvoy, Chris. 52
McEwen, John S. 51
McFarland, Armour 48
McFarland, Chas. H. 85
McFarland, Jas. 13
McFarlane, John 88
McFarlin, Thos. 62
McFeeters, Wm. L. 37
McGann, Michael A.
        77
McGarrity, John 46
McGee, Con 91
McGilligan, John 62
McGillycuddy, Val-
  entine T.(Dr.) 54
McGinnis, Daniel 52
McGinniss, Wm. 81
McGirr, Jas. 25
McGirr, Jas. J. 1
McGlone, Daniel 33
McGlone, John 40
McGlone, Michael 33
McGonigle, Hugh 35
McGowan, Martin 42
McGowan, Martin 23
McGrady, John 61
McGrail, Michael 56
McGraine, Michael
        77
McGrath, Daniel 64
McGrath, David 41
McGrath, Hugh 71
McGuiness, Wm. 81
McGuire, Edward 64
McGuire, John 31
McGurn, Bernard 26
McHugh, Frank 9
McIntee, Chas. 50
McIntyre, Chris. 67
McIntyre, Edward 49

McIntyre, Franklin
        J. 48
McKay, Edmond T. 35
McKee, Geo. 24
McKee, John 35
McKelery, Victor 16
McKenna, John 33
McKenna, Vincent 10
McKerr, Richard J. 75
McKibben, Jas. 10
McKiernan, Edward 76
McKnight, Geo. 69
McKnight, Jos. 56
McLain, Wm. 19
McLaughlin, Edward
        L. 60
McLaughlin, Hugh 24
McLaughlin, John 14
McLaughlin, Michael
        91
McLaughlin, Michael
        49
McLaughlin, Samuel
        23
McLaughlin, Terence
        30
McLaughlin, Thos.
        36
McLean, Hugh 86
McLennon, John 8
McLure, John 56
McMackin, Alfred 60
McMahon, Arthur 64
McMahon, Chas. 83
McMahon, Michael 79
McManus, Bernard 46
McManus, Wm. 69
McMasters, Wm. 30
McMath, Edmond 39
McMurray, Robt. 78
McNally, Jas. P. 37
McNamara, Jas. 36
McNamara, Michael
        52
McNamara, Thos. 76
McNamee, Eland (sp)
        63
McNeal, Frank 77
McNulty, Edward 62
McNulty, Jas. 44
McPartlen, Chas. 89
McPeak, Alex. 39
McQade, Jas. 64
McQuay, Michael 64

McTiernan, John 52
McVeigh, David 29
McWilliams, David 26.36
McShane, John 37
McShane, Paul 52
Madden, John 7
Madden, John 46
Madden, Wm. 65
Madden, Wm. 69
Madsen, Christian 56
Magee, Wm. 24
Magerlein, Marcus 76
Maginn, Frank 79
MAGUIRE, EDWARD 2
Maguire, Patrick I. 81
Maher, John 56
Maher, Martin 71,93
Maher, Thos. 83
Mahoney, Daniel 40
Mahoney, Daniel 86
Mahoney, John 31
Mains, John 1,25
Mains, Thos. J. 50
Maker, John 52
Malarkey, John 51
Malaw, Martin 57
Malcolm, Jean J. 17
Malcomson, Alex. 44
Malene, Patrick 46
Malentovic, Martin 57
Maley, John 23
Maley, Patrick 46
Maley, Patrick 63
Malin, Chas. 42
Malmiree, Edward 46
Maloney, Daniel 22
Maloney, John 45
Maloney, Miles 46
Maloney, Thos. 65
Mallis, Chas. 15
Malloy, Robt. C. 48
Malloy, Stephen 86
Manly, Jos. 74
Manning, David 32
Marbock, Jacob 57
Marcer, Henry 63
Marchand, Jos. 19
Maresh, John 44
Maricle, Franklin A. 73
Markham, Wm. 2,31
Marks, Adolph 52
Marler, Henry 67
Marlin, Michael 50
Marlow, Robt. 13

M

Maroney, Matt. 36
Marriaggi,Francis20
Marrion, Thos.C.71,
                    93
Marsh, Chas. 48
Marsh, Grant 1
  (Capt.:Far West)
Marshall, John S.61
Marshall, Wm.A. 32
Martin, Chas.H. 39
Martin, Edward 59
Martin, Geo. 52
Martin, Jas. 18
Martin, Jas. 79
Martin, John 36
Martin, John 78
Martin, John C. 8
Martin, John J. 31
Martin,Michael 32
Martin, Thos. 11
Martin, Wm. 30
Martin, Wm. B. 31
Martinak, Jas. 57
Martini, Gustav70
Martyn, Henry 33
MASON, JULIUS W.55
Mason,Samuel W. 56
Mason, Wm. 78
Mason, Wm. T. 53
Massingale,John D.
                    20
Massy, Hugh H. 81
Matcher,Eugene 92
Matheson, Neil 61
Mathews,Francis 41
Mathews, John 74
Mathews, Thos. 22
MATHEY, EDWARD G.4,
        28,31,40
Matthews, Geo. 11
Matthews, Wm.D. 11
Matza, John 42
Maua, Patrick 64
Mauch, Chas. 31
Maude, Chas.A. 67
Mauren, Jacob 17
Mautler, Taylor 64
Maybrook, Geo. 43
Mayer, Francis 73
Mayer, Fred. 80
Mayer, Jos. 62
Mayer, Wm. 20
Maynard, Arthur 53
Meadwell, John 32

Meagher, Peter 85
Meagher, Thos. 71
Mealy, Jacob 42
Meander, Herman 90
Mease, Levi H. 53
Meason, John 90
Mechlin,Henry W.B.
                    36
Meckel, Chas. 63
Medigar, Wm. 69
MEINHOLD, CHAS.66,73
Meier, John 13
Melbach, Oscar von56
Melin, Ernest 86
Mell, Henry 86
Melvill,David 14
Melville, Harry B.17
Mendhoff,Otto C.70
Menical, Frank 39
Meraker, Henry 64
Merkling,John 43
Merrill, John 61
Merritt,Andrew J.57
MERRITT, WESLEY 55
Merritt, Wm.H. 67
Meserole, David 84
Meyer, Fred. 6
Meyer, John 77
Meyering, Henry 58
Meyers, Frank 34
Meyers, Geo.S. 16
Meyers, John 32
Meyers, Wm. 20
Meysel, Geo. C. 8
Mezs (sp),Wolfgang
                    45
Middaugh, Samuel 24
Mier, Fred. F. 60
MICHAELIS, OTHO E.2
Michley, John W. 23
Mickler, Adam 34
Miles, Geo. 47
Miles, Jas. 40
MILES, NELSON A.3,
                    47
Miles, Wm. 60
Milink, Cyrus 56
Miller, August 85
Miller, Chas.(1) 20
Miller, Chas.(2) 20
Miller, Chas. 60
Miller, Chas. 62
Miller, Chas. 80
Miller, Chas.F.88

Miller, Geo. 52
Miller, Geo. 61
Miller, Geo. 89
Miller, Geo.F.W. 20
Miller, Henry 33
Miller, Jas. B. 81
Miller, Jas. C. 50
Miller, John 9
Miller, John 10
Miller, John 74
Miller, John 75
Miller, John 85
Miller, John H. 48
Miller, John M. 48
Miller, Jos. W. 57
Miller, Martin 11
Miller, Napoleon 21
Miller, Wm. 16
Miller, Wm. 76
Miller, Wm. 80
Miller, Wm. 84
Milligan, Louis P. 19
MILLS, ANSON 66,81
Mills, Cuthbert C. 54
Milner, Alfred 63
Milton, Jos. 34
Milwert, Otto 58
Minarcik, Chas. 71
Minchin, Michael G. 18
Minden. John 27
MINER, CHAS. W. 3,43
Miner, John 78
Minnehaw, Dennis 64
Minnick, John 37
Mitchell, Jas. 68
Mitchell, John 50
Mitchell, John J. 74
Mitchell, Reuben J.D.49
Moan, Peter 12
Moffitt, Wm. A. 69
Mohr, Jay 77
Mohrenstein,Chas. 89
Monach, Geo. 22
Monaghan,Peter E. 1,25
Monroe, Jas. C. 85
Monteeth,Abraham 90
Monteith, Victor 59
Montgomery, Jas. 76
MONTGOMERY, ROBT. H.55,57
Montgomery,Walter H. 51
Montrose, Chas. M. 52
Mooney, Thos. 59
Mooney, Wm. R. 18
Moore, Daniel 52

M

Moore, Henry 53
Moore, Hugh N. 40
Moore, Jas. 50
Moore, Jas. E. 30
Moore, Jas. M. 92
Moore, John 56
Moore, John 69
Moore, John G. 14
Moore, Lansing A.39
Moore,Martin M. 73
MOORE, ORLANDO H. 4
Moore, Robt. 91
Moore, Thos. 54
Moore, Wm. 6
Moore, Wm. 78
Moos, Henry 68
Morah, John 53
Moran, Jas. E. 6
Moran, John 71
Moran, Wm. 11
Morgan, Chas. 85
Morgan, Daniel 67
Morgan,Ezekial 83
Morgan, Geo.W. 2
Morgan, Jas. 88
Morgan, John 59
Morgan, Jos.W. 81
Morganthaler,Albert
                    81
Moriarity, John 73
Moriarity,Patrick61
Morris, Chas. R. 2
Morris,Michael 22
Morrison, Chas. 71
Morrison, John 35
Morrow, Jas. 62
Morrow, Wm. E. 30
Morsell, Jas. 56
Morton, Edward 80
Morton, Chas. 42
MORTON, CHAS. 66,72
Morton, Edward 89
Morton, Frank D. 6
Morton, Jas. A. 85
Morton, Thos. 32
Mosher, Henry 85
Mosier,Solomon 50
Mott, Wm. H. 50
Moulton, Eugene 62
Moushart, Maxmilian
                    92
MOYLAN, MYLES 4,28,
                    29

Mueller, Wm. 32
Muering, John 29
Muessigbrodt,Chas.
                    22
Mulcahy, Edward 9
Mulcahy, Patrick 19
Mulhern, Wm. J. 25
Mullane, Denis 92
Mullen, John 39
Muller, Chas. 20
Muller, Chas. 80
Muller, Ernest 59
Mulligan, Frank 31
Mulligan, Geo. 4
Mulligan, John 48
Mullin, Martin 31
Mullins, Chris. 91
Mulvey, Jas. 74
Mundlay, Jas. 34
Munger, Daniel 67,93
Munn, Fred M. 17
Munschey, Chrisoston
                    44
Munson, Chas. R. 45
MUNSON, SAMUEL 82,86
MURDOCK, DANIEL H.
                    3,23
Murname, Thos. 56
Murphy, Andrew 86
Murphy, Ben. 92
Murphy, Daniel 53
Murphy, David 17
Murphy, Edward L. 90
Murphy, Frank 7
Murphy,Hamilton B.61
Murphy,Lawrence 33
Murphy,Jeremiah 77
Murphy,Jeremiah 81
Murphy, John 67
Murphy, John 77
MURPHY, JOHN 82,90
Murphy, John D. 64
Murphy, John J. 52
Murphy,Michael 38
Murphy,Michael 87
Murphy,Nicholas 12
Murphy,Patrick 22
Murphy,Patrick 45
Murphy,Patrick 57
Murphy, Robt. L.37
Murphy, Thos. 38
Murphy, Thos. 41
Murphy, Thos. 59

Murray, Chas. 16
Murray, Henry 38
Murray, Jas. 18
Murray, Jas. 49
Murray, John 61
Murray, Jos. 60
Murray, Julius 73
Murray, Michael 39
Murray, Michael 51
Murray, Thos. 30
Murray, Thos. 61
Murray, Thos. 68
Murray, Wm. C. 70
Muster,Nicholas 34
Myers, Fred. 37
Myers, John 62
Myers, Samuel 62
Myers, Wm. 20
Myls, Jas. 37


N


Naaf, John 67
Nagle, Edward 70
Nagles, John 36
Nail, Kermit G. 15
Napoleon, Chas. 33
Navarra, Eugene 11
Navarre, Oliver 86
Nealon, Daniel 36
Neel, Robt. 79
Neely, Frank 40
Neerey, Chas. 46
Nees, Edler 36
Neibuhr, Wilhelm 58
Neiderst,Florence 72
Neil, David W. 67
Neiss, John H. 84
Nelon, Leander 34
Nelson, Henry 58
Nelson, John R. 14
Netherly, Wm. 58
Neurohr, Jos. 76
Newman, Edward 62
Newman, John G. 87
Nicholas, Joshua S. 36
Nichols, Chas. A. 86
Nichols, Fulton A. 20
NICKERSON, JAS. D. 19
Nicolai, Gustavus 69
Nieschang, Louis R. 20
Nihill, John 61
Niles, Francis S. 89

N

Nitsche, Ottocar 31
Nobles, Wm. 88
Noblette,Lewis A.51
Nolan, Edward 44
Nolan, Jas. 74
Nolan, John 38
Nolan, Matthew 90
Nolan, Peter 89
Nolan, Thos. 18
Nolan, Thos. 76
Noonan, Jas. 56
Noonan, Patrick 51
Noonan, Robt. 67
Noonan, Wm. 10
Nordegeski, Haymes
        (sp) 63
North, Jas. H. 56
North, Walter A.60
Northeg, Orlaus 35
Norton, Jas. 9
Norton, John 87
Norvell, Thos. F.80
Norwood, Wm. F. 67
Noteman, Alex. 77
NOWLAN, HENRY J. 2
NOYES, HENRY E.66,
            71
Nugent, Wm. D. 29
Nunan, John 27
  (see Minden also)
Nunemaker, Amos 61
Nunke, Albert 58


O

Oakley, Chas. N.31
Oaks, Geo. B. 80
O'Brien, Dennis 42
O'Brien, Edward 41
O'Brien, Jas. 79
O'Brien,Jeremiah 62
O'Brien, John 45
O'Brien, John D. 84
O'Brien, Martin 53
O'BRIEN, M. EDWARD
            66,67
O'Brien, Michael 92
O'Brien, Terence 20
O'Brien, Thos.26
O'Connell, Jas. 41
O'Conner, John 17
O'Connor, Edward 51
O'Connor,Francis 68

O'Connor, John 51
O'Connor, John 62
O'Connor,Patrick 44
O'Connors, John 18
Odell, Francis A. 61
O'Donnell, Jas. 80
O'Donnell,Michael 51
O'Donnell, Peter 24
O'Donnell, Wm. 43
Odeu, Chas. 19
O'Flynn, John J. 14
O'Grady, Gerold J.77
O'Grady, Richard 77
O'Hearn, Richard 88
O'Hearne,Michael 77
Ohm, Gustav 71
O'Keefe, Thos. I.81
O'Kelly, Jas. J. 2
Oldsworth, Thos.F.21
Olsson, Henry 78
Olstad, Chas. 50
O'Mahon, Henry 33
O'Malley,Anthony 51
O'Malley, Thos. 10
O'Mann, Wm. 32
O'Neil, Henry 56
O'Neil, Jas. 65
O'Neil, Jas. H. 76
O'Neil, Jesse 51
O'Neill,Bernard 26
O'Neill, Jas. 39
O'Neill, Jas. 50
O'Neill, Jas. 60
O'Neill, Jas. I.45
O'Neill, John 30
O'Neill, John 49
O'Neill, Thos. 35
O'Rielley,Michael 79
Ormann, Rudolph 87
Orr, Chas. D. 33
Orr, Chas. M. 26
Orrington,Richard 12
Ort, Daniel 65
Osborn, Wm. G. 15
Osgood, Frank E. 20
O'Shaughnessy, Thos.
            51
Osmer, Wm. C. 14
Osterday, Gottlieb
            78
O'Sullivan, Jas. 53
O'Sullivan, John 14
O'Sullivan,Richard 84

O'Sullivan, Thos. 92
O'Sullivan,Timothy 87
OTIS, ELWELL S. 3
O'Toole, Francis 33
Ott, John 58
OVENSHINE, SAMUEL 3,
            47,51
Overton, Chas. 37
Owens, Eugene 37
Owens, John 53
Owens, Patrick 41


P

Page, Edward 17
Palle, Adano 64
Palmer, Frank A. 31
Palmer, Wm. M. 25
Pandtle, Chris. 33
Pangborn, John 21
PARDEE, JULIUS H. 55
Paris, Wm. H. 34
Parker, Chas. E. 69
Parker, Edgar W. 9
Parker, Wm. S. 14
PARKHURST, CHAS. D.
            55,60
Parks, Jas. L. 80
Parle, John 42
Parnell, Thos. 20
Parrington,Richard 70
Parrum, John D. 56
Parsons, Wm. S. 86
Partridge,Michael 11
Patrick, Jos. B. 59
Patterson, Geo. W. 65
Patterson, Jas. 56
Patterson, Jos. 76
Patterson,Roswell E.80
Patton, John 72
PATZKI, JULIUS H.(Dr.)
            54
PAUL, AUGUSTUS C. 66,81
Paul, Fred. 74
Paul, Wm. F. 70
Paulding, Holmes O.(Dr.)
            2
Payne, Francis 50
PAYNE, JOHN S. 55,61
Payne, Rosell W. 69
Pearson, Clifford 16
PEARSON, DANIEL C.66,67
Pease, Wm. 76

P

Peck, Geo. W.A. 59
Peffer, Andrews 15
Penney, Eugene H.37
Pennington, Jas. 51
Penwell, Geo. B. 38
Penwell, John S. 48
Perkins, Henry 76
Perkins, Jas. 74
Perkins, John H. 19
Pernell, Julius 88
Perry, Wm. 83
Perry, Geo. 15
Perry, Linden B. 70
Perry, Wm. 83
Peshall,Richard W.51
Peters,Samuel D. 85
Petit, John 20
Peterson,Samuel 72
Peterson, Walter 61
Petrie, Philip 46
Petring, Henry 35
Pettibone,Claude M.
                    57
Phelan, Robt. W. 49
Phelan, Thos. 78
Phillips,Francis 16
Phillips, John 75
Phillips, John J.19
Phillips,Nathan B.
                    52
Phister, Louis 80
Pickard, Edwin H.34
Pickens, Wm. 60
Pier, Ernest 50
Pigford, Edward 40
Pilcher,Albert 34
Pilkington,Patrick
                    79
Pilts, Carl 5
Pinkston, John S.36
Pippher, Jacob 23
Pivina,Maurice L.63
Plant, Samuel 8
Pliuker, Gerrit 45
Plum, Emil 17
PLUMMER,SATTERLEE C.
                 55,63
Plunkett, Thos. 19
Poetling, Edward 9
Polk, Wheeler H.15
Pomeroy, Noah G.13
Pommer, John 63
Pool, Chas. A. 91

POOLE, DEWITT C.
                  3,44
Poole, Sylvester 88
Pope, Jas. A. 50
POPE, JAS. W.3,47,
                    49
Pope, John C. 60
Poppe, John A. 61
Porter, Henry (Dr.)
                    2
Porter, Wm.J. 67
Post, Fred. 58
Potter, John 48
Potts, Wm. H. 60
Pourier, Baptiste
('Big Bat') 54,93
POWELL, JAS. W.3,22
Powell, Junius L.54
POWELL, WM. H.82,85
Power, Wm. H. 6
Powers, Geo. 49
Powers, Jas. 53
Powers, John 56
Powers,Patrick 33
Powers, Thos. 21
Pratt, Robt. F. 79
Pratt,Timothy H.49
Pregler, Louis 50
Prentice, Geo. W.15
Prescott, Eli 19
Press, John 64
PRICE, GEORGE F.55,
                    60
Priest, Robt. H.63
Prince,Eugene M.80
Pringle, Adam 81
Procter, Henry 58
Proctor, Geo. H.29
Prosper,Antoine 41
Prutting, John F.
                    17
Pulli, Chas. H. 75
Puryear, Adolf 14
Putnam, Danny 39
Putnam, John C. 69
Pym, Jas. 30


Q

Quado, Frank 74
Quidde, Robt. 89
Quiena,Richard 51
Quigley, Chas. 65

Quigley, Jas. 51
Quinlan, John 34
Quinlaw, Michael 91
Quinn, Henry L. 73
Quinn, Jas. 76
Quinn, John 32
Quinn, Thos. 60
Quinn, Thos. 78

R

Raab, Geo. 81
Radcliff, Jas. 90
Radcliff, Miles A. 49
Rafferty, John 8
Rafferty, John 10
Rafferty, John C. 87
Rafter, John 38
Ragan, Michael 38
Ragsdale, John 26
Raichel, Henry W. 38
Rall, Julius 41
Ralph, Thos. 12
Ramell, Wm. 36
Ramer, Jas. 68
Ramey, Martin 23
Ramsey, Chas. 37
Ramsome, Calvin 86
Ramston, Henry 72
Rance, Thos. W. 19
RANDALL, EDWARD L.47,50
Randall, Geo. F. 30
RANDALL, GEORGE M.54
Randall, Jas. 7
Randall, Wm. J. 32
Randolph, Chas. 22
Ransom, Delos 89
Rapp, Jacob F. 55
Raston, Geo. 37
Rathmann, Henry 44
Rauden, August 64
Raw, August 10
Rawcliffe, Alfero 75
RAWOLLE, WILLIAM C.66,68
Ray, Fred. 78
Ray, Geo. 80
Ray, Jas. H. 71
Ray, Wm. 79
Reader, Jas. 11
Reap, Martin 9
Reardon, Alex. 76
Reardon,Cornelius 87
Reardon, John 16

Redd, Jas. E. 24
Reddy, Daniel P. 88
Redmond, Peter J. 68
Rednor, Webster 23
Reed, Edward F. 42
Reed, John 74
Reed, John A. 35
Reed, Willard E. 43
Reed, Wm. 45
REED, WILLIAM I. 10
Reese, Wm. 33
Reeves, Edward 50
Reeves, John R. 50
Regan, Wm. L.67,93
Regien, Geo. 58
Rehberg, Geo. 84
Reid, Chas. 83
Reid, Elwyn S. 32
Reid, Philip 9
Reid, Thos. 46
Reilley, Chris.T.85
Reilley, Michael 34
REILLY, BERNARD JR.
            55,63
Reilly, John 72
Reilly, Michael 38
Reilly, Patrick 64
Reilly, Reuben 1
Reilly, Wm. 49
Rein, Francis 11
Reis, August 22
Remley, Oliver 70
Remy, John 59
Renear, Dave C. 81
Renner, Emile 69
RENO, MARCUS A.4,28
Reppert, John W. 74
Ressel, Geo. 65
Reuter, Jos. 65
Revenew, Wm. H. 91
REYNOLDS, BAINBRIDGE
            66,77
Reynolds, John 53
Reynolds, John 71
Reynolds, John L.12
Reynolds, Michael 67
Reynolds, Wm. H. 81
Rhinehart, Jos. 1
Rhode, Geo. 71,93
RICE, EDMUND 3,47,
                52
Rice, Henry 7
Rice, Robt. 73
Rice, Wm. 76
Rich, Herbert S. 89

Richards, Jas. 51
Richardson, Jas.H.
                59
Richaud, Louis 54
Richner, Isaac 85
Richon, John F.51
Ricketts, Jos. 27
Riden, Ansil 17
Riech, Max 88
Rieder, Fred. A.48
Rielley, Jas. 79
Rielly, Mathew 92
Rigney, Michael 12
Riley, Thos. 53
Riley, Thos. 56
Riley, Thos. 75
Riley, Wm. 74
Ring, Dennis 24
Rintz, Philip 92
Riordan, Wm. 53
Ritchart, Wm. 20
Ritchie, John 73
Rivers, Frank 83
Rivers, Geo. 11
Rivers, Geo. 21
Rivers, John 27
Roach, Hampton M.
                61
Robb, Eldorado I.35
Robers, Jonathan 38
Roberts, Aquilla 50
Roberts, Chas. 24
Roberts, Jas.L.72
Roberts, Jas.P.58
Roberts, John M. 63
Roberts, Robt. 79
Roberts, Wm. 61
Robertson, Chas.M.
                33
Robertson, Cody 70
ROBERTSON, EDGAR B.
                82,88
Robertson, Walter S.
                10
Robideau, Maxim 17
Robinson, Chas. V.
                63
Robinson, David 23
Robinson, Franklin
              B. 81
Robinson, Geo.B.
              67,93
Robinson, John 44
Robinson, Jos. 65
Robinson, Jos. 75

Robinson, Thaddeus 90
Robinson, Wm. 21
Robinson, Wm. 40
Robinson, Wm. W. 75
Roche, Morris 7
ROCKEFELLER, CHAS. M.
              82,88
ROCKWELL, CHAS. H. 55
RODGERS, CALBRAITH P.
              55,56
Rodgers, Francis 74
Rodgers, Jas. 62
Rodgers, Jas. W. 23
ROE, CHARLES FRANCIS 4,14
Roehm, Emil 50
Roett, John G. 31
Rogers, Geo. 6
Rogers, Thos. 20
Rogers, Wm. F. 61
Rohrs, John F.C. 55
Roisvetter, Chas. 63
Rollan, Oscar 70
Roller, Wm. 7
Rollins, Wm. T. 56
ROMEYN, HENRY 47,48
Roof, Ross H. 58
Rooney, Edward 53
Rooney, Jas.M. 34
Roper, Herbert 34
Roper, Ludwig 84
Ropetsky, Frank 75
Rose, Jas.E. 78
Rose, Peter E. 39
Rosenberry, Allen J.78
Rosenburger, John 90
Rosendale, Geo. 70
Ross, Albert 11
Ross, Daniel C. 76
Ross, Geo. 39
Rotchford, Jas. 15
Roth, Francis 38
Roth, John M. 52
Rott, Louis 38
Roulston, Robt. 73
Rowbee, Geo.W. 68
Rowland, Robt. 35
Rowsell, Geo. W. 84
Roy, Stanislaus 29
ROYALL, WILLIAM B. 66
Rozell, Jos. B. 84
Ruckesback, Albert 57
Rudden, Patrick 11
Rudolph, Geo. 26
Rue, Mark B. 68
Ruf, Gottlieb 71

R

Ruffle, Chas. W. 78
Ruffner, Simon C.60
Rufus,Valentine70,93
Rugg, Frank 77
Ruiz, Frank 91
Ruland, Frank 16
Russell, Chas. 54
Russell, Geo. W. 61
Russell, John 71
Russell, Thos. 32
Russell, Thos. 89
Ruth, John 15
Rutten,Ferdinand 77
Ryan, Andrew 41
Ryan, David 51
Ryan, Jas. 17
Ryan, John 40
Ryan, John 56
Ryan, Jos. 50
Ryan,Michael 48
Ryan, Patrick 79
Ryan, Patrick H.49
Ryan, Stephen L.30
Ryan, Wm. O. 36
Ryder, Hobart 40
Ryder, Jas. 43
Rye, Wm. W. 40


S


Sachs, Louis 74
Sadler, Wm. 32
Saffell, Thos.O.49
Sager, Hiram W. 30
Sagle, Wm. F. 22
Salice, Albert 77
Salmon, Thos. 64
Salzner, Gustave 41
Samuel, Bernard 91
Sanders, Chas. 32
Sanders, Fred. P.65
Sanders, John F. 75
Sanders, Thos. 24
Sanders, Wm.H. 10
Sanderson,Geo.E. 74
Sanderson, Jas. 17
Sands, Edward H. 49
Sands, Jas. 64
Sandy, John W. 83
Sanford, Jos. 13
Sanford, Thos.D.73
Sanford,Wilmot P.
                    23

SANGER, LOUIS H.4,20
SANNO, JAS.M.J. 3,13
Sargent, Chas. H. 70
Sarratt, John 18
Sartain, Wm.A. 25
Sarven, John H. 14
Savelle, Philip 42
Scanlon, Peter 12
Schalgen, Rochus 85
Schardun, Albert 50
Schargenstein,Henry
                    16
Schedwick,Theodore
                    57
Schenberg, Heinrich
                    58
Schenkberg, Antony
                    80
Schimpoff, Emil 60
Schindler,Edward 51
Schlacker, Jos. 60
Schlafer, Chris. 38
Schleiforth, Paul 34
Schlieper, Claus 34
Schmalz, Blaseus 81
Schmid, Fred. 56
Schmid, Konrad 71
Schmidt, Chas. 48
Schmidt, Claud 80
Schmidt, Edward 57
Schmidt, Ernest 51
Schmidt, Henry 78
Schmidt, Jos. 50
Schmidt, Martin 56
Schmidtt, Jos. 81
Schmitz, Mathias 64
Schnable,Bernard 67
Schneider,August 58
Schneider, Paul 65
Schneiderhan,Lawrence
                    83
SCHOFIELD, CHAS.B.
                 5,17
Schomberg, August 24
Schon, Julius 45
Schopp, Jos. 50
Schott, Wm. 42
Schreiber, Edmund 64
Schreiner,Henry E.13
Schubert, Wm. 76
Schubert, Wm. 79
Schucks,Augustus 46
Schumaker,Jacob 84

Schuster, Michael 51
Schuttle, Fred. 81
SCHUYLER, WALTER S.54
Schwab, Chas. 25
SCHWATKA,FREDERICK66,81
Schweigert, Jos. 48
Schweikart, Peter 78
Schweiker, Julius 56
Schweitzer, John 46
Schwerer, John 38
Scollin, Jas. 43
Scott, Henry 11
Scott, Geo.D. 32
Scott, Jas. 48
Scott, Jas. A. 70
Scott, John 25
Scott, Joshua 83
Scott, Thos. 10
Scott, Wm. 18
Scottin, Wm. M. 58
Scribner, Wm. H. 92
Scully, Patrick 76
Seadorf, Alfred 89
Seamans, John 40
Seamon, Walter 20
Seaver, Fred. 22
Seayers, Thos. 29
Secord, Thos. A. 67
Secrist, Frank P. 76
Seegar, Herman 48
Seekange, Henry 56
Seery, John 88
Segman, Archy T. 11
Seibert, Edward 14
Selden, Walter 12
Semmber, Chas. 53
Semple, John 77
Senn, Robt. 40
Senni, Chas. 89
Serfas, Frank 81
Server, Fred. E. 15
SETON, HENRY 82,83
Seuter, Chas. J. 61
Severs, Jas. 40
Shaddock, Jos. 63
Shafer, Henry 72
Shanahan, John 35
Shanley, Jas. 81
Shannon, Bart. 68
Shannon, Jas. 43
Shannon, Martin 17
Sharlett, Jas. 18
Sharron, John 62

S

Shauer, John 38
Shaw, Eli 31
Shaw, Fred. W. 65
Shaver, John 28
Shay, John 60
Shea,Cornelius 90
Shea, Daniel 30
Shea, Thos. 48
Sheehan, John 52
Sheehan. Geo. 81
Shepler, Frank 19
Sheppard, Chris.57
Shepperson,Fuller H.
              80
Sherbon, Thos. 26
Sheridan, John 85
Sherman,John H.74
Sherry, Wm.J. 65
Shields, Andrew 92
Shields, Daniel 79
Shields, Dennis 51
Shields, Jas. 21
Shields,Jeremiah 46
Shields, John 69
Shields, Henry 85
Shields,Peter D. 59
Shields, Wm. 33
Shiffer, Eugene C.48
Shine, Daniel F. 63
Shipp, Wm. F. 49
Shire, Alex. 76
Shortis, Benj.F. 24
Shuless, Geo. 14
Shultz, Robt. 39
Shurhammer, Frank 87
Shutte, Fred. 34
Sibbeske, Geo. 14
SIBLEY,FREDERICK W.
        66,69,93
Sidelinger, Remly 39
Siebelder, Anton 29
Sieber, Fred. 48
Siefert, August 38
Sieffert, Conrad 18
Siglock, Ernest 50
Simmons, Geo. 44
Simon, Chas. 22
Simon, Wm. 13
Simons, Albert 72
Simons, Patrick 30
Simmonson, Hans 58
Simonson, Julius 25
SIMPSON,JAS.F.66,73,
          75

Simpson, Thos. 67
Sims, John S. 32
Singer, John W. 81
Singleton, Lewis 79
Sinsil, Jos. C. 6
Sipes, Jas. 1
Sipfler, Chris. 6
Sivertson, John 40
Skehan, Wm. F. 41
Skinner, Wm. 71
Slaper, Wm. 40
Slater, Thos. 73
Sloan,David O. 74
Sloan, Jas. 57
Sloan, Oscar 84
Slocum, Chas.S.87
Slough, John P. 71
Sluiky (sp),Michael
              61
Small, John R. 35
SMEAD, ALEX. D.B.66,
              77
Smiley, Thos.R. 23
Smith, Aaron 88
Smith, Alex F. 19
Smith, Alfred 83
Smith, Calvin 12
Smith, Chas. 19
Smith, Chas. 50
Smith, Chas. F. 78
Smith, Chas. M. 55
Smith, Edward R. 45
SMITH, EDWARD W. 2
Smith, Francis 79
Smith, Frank 46
Smith, Frank 65
Smith, Frank 73
Smith, Franklin A.
              83
Smith, Fred. 38
Smith, Fred. W. 22
Smith, Geo. 85
Smith, Geo. C. 6
Smith, Geo. M. 60
Smith, Henry 9
Smith, Henry G. 32
Smith, Henry J. 22
Smith, Hugh 44
Smith, Jacob 24
Smith, Jas. 70
Smith, Jas. H. 35
Smith, Jos. 8
Smith, John 24

Smith, John 58
Smith, John 61
Smith, John 65
Smith, John 78
Smith, John 88
Smith, John 89
Smith, John 92
Smith, John II 79
Smith, John A. 74
Smith, John B. 8
Smith, John F. 56
Smith, John H. 46
Smith, John H. 73
Smith, John T. 80
Smith, Malcolm 64
Smith, Orson M. 70
SMITH, OSKALOOSA M.44
Smith, Peter 61
Smith, Rhinehart 83
Smith, Robt. 81
Smith, Samuel 87
Smith, Vic 2
Smith, Walter C. 86
Smith, Wm. 43
Smith, Wm. 58
Smith, Wm. 78
Smith, Wm. E. 32
Smith, Wm. G. 21
Smith, Wm. H. 86
Smithson, Sidney 46
Smolinski,Anthony 85
Smyth, John 41
Snepp, Jas. E. 72
Snider, Geo. 59
Sniffin, Frank 40
Snow, Elmer A. 81
Snow, Eugene 19
Snowden, Harry 74
Snyder, Robt. O. 57
SNYDER, SIMON 3,47,50
Soffine,Adolf von 2,31
Soltneider, Henry C. 22
Somers, Robt. 15
Somers, Wm. F. 14
Somers, Wm. F. 67
Sorden, Thos. 35
Soule, Geo. A. 80
Southon, Alfred S. 72
Spalding, Collomb 10
Spalding, John F. 19
Spalding,Samuel P. 90
Spangenberg, Hiram 42
Spangler, Basil S. 85

S

Sparks, Peter 34
Spayd, Isaac H. 8
Spearman, Frank 92
Speckman, John 85
Speirs, John 19
Spencer, Able B. 33
Spencer, Chas. 67
Spencer, Samuel M.56
Spinner, Philip 30
Spitser, David 51
Spreight, Geo. 78
Spring, Edward T.18
Sproul, Geo. 80
Sproul, Robt. 19
Spurgeon, Geo. S.88
Stacy, Geo. T. 91
Stafford, Jos. 50
Stahl, Francis 75
Stakley, Jacob 62
Staley, Isaac 49
Staley, John 77
Stanford, Thos. F.13
Stanley, John 20
Stanley, Samuel 76
Stanton, Edward 60
STANTON,THADDEUS H.
                    54
Starck, Frank 26
Stark, Albert 65
Stark, Jas. 63
Starke, Chas. W.85
Starr, Daniel C.14
Stauffer,Rudolph 64
Stavnois, Jas. 57
St.Clair, Francis M.
                    56
Stearns, Lucius E.84
Steckham, Peter 42
Steele, Francis A.20
Steele, Geo. 74
Steiger, Frank J.49
Stein, C.A. 26
Stein, Geo. 11
Steine, Geo. 75
Steiner, Henry 73
Steintker,John R.38
Stendla, Jacob 64
Stephanic, Jas. 57
Stephens, Chas.R.54
Stephens, David 61
Stephens, Geo. W.35
Stephenson,John 88
Sterland,Walter S.40

Stevens, Chas. 6
Stevens, Geo. W. 51
Stevens, John 31
Stevens, John 75
Stevens, Wm. 92
Stevenson, John I.
                    81
Stevenson, John M.
                    71
Stevenson, Thos.35
Steward, Chas. W.41
Stewart, Benj.F. 10
Stewart, Chas.H. 19
Stewart, Daniel 60
Stewart,Francis 16
Stewart, Jas. 62
Stewart, Jas. 65
Stewart, Wm. 74
Stickney, Geo. 73
Stieffel,Herman 53
Stierle, Charlie 24
Stilwell, Wm. 84
Stinger, John 83
Stivers, Thos.W. 32
Stoffel, Henry 39
Stoll, Henry 88
Stollnow, Chas. 83
Stone, Geo. A.69,93
Stone, Henry A. 33
Stone, Levi A. 23
Stone, Watson P. 15
Storm, Hans 22
Stortz, Fred. 7
Stout, Edward 30
Stout, Irvine H. 71
Stoy,Garrison L. 33
Stoy, Henry W. 33
Strahorn, Robt.E.54
Strait, John W. 63
Strang, Albion R.91
Strang, Geo.T. 91
Stratton, Frank 40
Street, David 20
Striber, Louis 9
Strickert, Fritz 79
Stritten,Michael 13
Strohm, Caspar 19
Strut, John 92
Sttuka, John J. 25
Stuart, Chas. 63
Stuart, Chas. W.79
Stumpf, Edward 8
Sturm, Jos. 41

Sturm, Robt. 6
Sullivan, Daniel 35
Sullivan, Dennis 75
Sullivan, Jas. M. 90
Sullivan,Jeremiah 64
Sullivan, John 42
Sullivan, John 45
Sullivan, John 49
Sullivan, John 79
Sullivan, Jos. 63
Sullivan, Martin 7
Sullivan, Michel 80
Sullivan, Patrick 8
Sullivan, Patrick 70
SUMNER, SAMUEL S. 55,59
Sutcliffe, Fred. 58
SUTORIUS, ALEXANDER 76
Swain, Wm. 84
Sweeney, Geo. W. 67
Sweeney, Jas. 73
Sweeney, John 81
Sweeney, John W. 34
SWIGERT, SAMUEL M. 66,69


T

Taggart, Jas. 72
Tailor, Wm. H. 68
Talbot, J.J. 54
Taska, Fred. 84
Taube, Emil 27
Tausher, Chas. 70
Tavlane, John 6
Taylor,(Dr.) Blair
   or Marcus (?) 2
Taylor, Chas. 75
TAYLOR, FRANK 82,92
Taylor, John A. 78
Taylor,'Muggins' 2
Taylor, Richard 83
Taylor, Walter O. 35
Taylor, Warren 88
Taylor, Wm. 78
Taylor, Wm. 71
Taylor, Wm. 91
Taylor, Wm. O. 29
Taylor, Wm. S. 61
Teeple, Ralph 53
Teeters, Samuel E. 23
Ten Eyck, Jas. 59
Tenni, Peter 12
Tepe, John B. 50
TERRY, ALFRED H. 2

T

Terry, John H. 83
Tesson, Louis (Dr.) 2,
                    47
Tetner, August E. 64
Tevaddeli, Alex. 53
Texton, John 61
Thalon, Jos. 24
Thealman, Chas. 57
Therion, Ernest 72
Thianich, Geo.von 6
THIBAUT, FREDERICK W.
            23,25
Thiele, Geo. W. 42
Thilman, Augustus 83
Thomas, Frank 37
Thomas, Frank H. 19
Thomas, Jas. 30
Thomas, John 87
Thomas, Lewis 90
Thompson,Augustus 68
Thompson, Ben 1
Thompson, Edward 56
Thompson, Henry C. 49
Thompson, Hugh C. 19
Thompson, Jas. 57
Thompson, John 17
THOMPSON, LEWIS 17
THOMPSON, RICHARD E.2
Thompson, Wm. 12
Thompson, Wm. 17
Thomson, Hugh 87
Thomson, Samuel P. 59
Thorison, John H. 73
Thornberry, Levi 40
Thornton, Richard 22
Thorpe, Rollini L.40
Tierney, Andrew 74
Tierson, Benj. F. 62
Tigerstroem, Otto 80
Tighe, John 73
Till, Peter 89
Tilson, David A. 73
Tilton, Frank 39
Timmey, Daniel 76
Tinkham, Henry L. 30
Tischer, John 77
Tobey, Fred. H. 39
TOBEY, THOMAS F.82,91
Tobin, Patrick 41
Tobin, Robt. 58
Todd, Jas. F. 80
Tolan, Frank 32
Tomlinson, Frank 51

Tooel, Patrick 78
Torman, Carlton 69
Tothamer, Ole 86
Towne, Phineas 77
Tracy, Chas. 80
Tracy, Gamaliel 59
Traubman, Jacob 37
Traynor, Jim 93
Tredick, Chas. E.
                81
Tresh, Geo. H. 37
Tritten, John G.26
Trotvine,Philip 20
Trumble, Wm. 30
Tucker, Henry N.73
Tud, Byron 57
Tully, Thos. 1,25
Tulo, Jos. 35
Turner, Jos. 84
Turner, Jos. A. 85
Turnholt, Thos. 14
Twiggs,Jeremiah 70
Tyler, Franklin 51
Tyler, Geo. 92
Tyler, Horace 57

U

Ulitz, Arthur 48
Unger, John 50
UPHAM, JOHN V. 55

V

Valentine, Chas.45
Van Ardenne,Peter T.
              R. 10
Van Arnim, Julius 26
Vance, Jas. 70
Vance, Wm. H. 72
Van Horn, Abraham 45
Van Houton, Harry 92
Van Moll, John W. 72
Van Pelt, Wm. A. 27
Van Seer, Azabel R.80
Van Vert, Albert 46
VAN VLIET, FREDERICK
              66,74
Varney, Averius S.77
VARNUM, CHARLES A.37
Very, Soren O. 81
Vickers, Chas. H. 49
Vickers, Geo. D. 68

Viele, Stephen S. 85
Vinatieri, Felix V.26
Vincent, Alonzo A. 67
Vincent, John F. 67
Vincent, John W. 67
Vogle, Wernard 48
Voit, Otto 36
Volker, John 90
VOLKMAR, WILLIAM J. 57
Vollinger, Jacob 50
Volmer, Wm. 70
VON LUETTWITZ, ADOLPHUS
              66,74,76
Von Thianich, Geo. 6
Vreeland, Geo. H. 32
VROOM, PETER D. 66,80

W

Waag, Peter 70
Wadr, Nicholas 52
Wadsworth, Jos. A. 69
Wagner, Albert 83
Wagner, Hugo 70
Wahler, Louis 24
Wait, Geo. B. 90
Waitsour, Leon 64
Walcott, Wm. M. 74
Waldo, John L. 19
Walker, Edward 80
Walker, Geo. 24
WALKER, GEORGE B.3,24
WALKER, HENRY P. 2,20
Walker, Jas. E.A. 43
Walker, Robt. 31
Walker, Robt. H. 61
Walker, Thos. 80
Wall, Geo. S. 14
Wall, Patrick 68
Wall, Patrick H. 71
WALLACE, GEORGE D. 28,
              34,35
Wallace, John 64
Wallace, John W. 35
Wallace, Richard A. 30
Wallace, Robt. 53
Wallace, Samuel 10
Wallace, Thos. 14
Wallen, Morris 50
Waller, Jos. 14
Walsh, Daniel 71
Walsh, Jas. 7
Walsh, John 88

W

Walsh, Jas. 67
Walsh, John 24
Walsh, John 33
Walsh, Michael 88
Walsh, Richard 16
Walsh, Robt. 53
Walsh, Thos. 34
Walsh, Wm. H. 42
Walter, Aloyse L.26,
                36
Walter, Geo. 52
Walter,Samuel J. 48
Walter, Wm. 8
Walters, Chas. 11
Walters, Frank 16
Walters, Geo.J. 71
Walton, John 44
Walton, Wm. 73
Waltz, Fred. 33
Waltz,Sylvester 9
Walzer, Jos. 81
Wanamaker,Ben A. 63
Ward, Arthur 17
Ward, Chas. 75
Ward, Jas. 41
Ward, John 53
Ward, Jos.69,93
Ward, Hugh B. 53
Ward, Louis F. 48
Ward, Maurice 20
Ward, Wm. 64
Warfield, John C.A.
                77
Warner, John C. 24
Warren, John 49
Warren, John B. 16
Warrington,Henry E.
                69
Washakie, Chief 54
Wasmus, Ernest 38
Wasson, Jos. 54
Waterhouse, Wm. 90
Waters, Jas. 88
Waters, Patrick 33
Watson,Edward A. 69
Watson, Jas. 31
Watson, Jas. A. 6
Watson, Henry 14
Watson, Hugh J. 39
Watson, Wm. H. 53
WATTS, CHARLES 65
Watts, Geo. 71,93
Watts, Wm. J. 63
Waugh, Chas. 92

Weaver, Geo. 40
Weaver, Henry C.40
Weaver, Herbert W.79
Weaver, Howard H. 29
Weaver, Isaac 48
Weaver, John A. 62
Webb, Henry O. 64
Webb, Jacob R. 75
Webb, Wm. T. 69
Webb, Wm. L. 69
Webber, Chas. 6
Weber, Arnold 74
Weber, August 9
Weber, Fred. 75
Weber, John 56
Webster, Chas. 80
Webster, J.Franklin
                75
Weed, Wm. F. 53
Weekoft, Peter 64
Weeks, Jas. 40
Weeks, John A. 90
Wegman, Barney 51
Weidaw, John 43
Weidman, John 39
Weierbach,Aaron T.
                23
Weil, Julius B. 57
Weiler, Adolf 41
Weir, Hugh 61
WEIR, THOMAS B.4,28,
                32
Weis, Jos. 5
Weise, Fred. 53
Weiss, Henry 51
Weiss, Marcus 35
Welch, Chas. H. 32
Welch, John 58
Welch, Thos. 79
Wells, Chas. 53
Wells, Edward 16
WELLS, ELIJAH R. 66,
                70
Wells, Jas. 83
Wells, Peter 53
Wells, Walter 72
Wellwood, Henry 74
Welsh, Edward 9
Welsh, Jas. 78
Welsh, John 74
Wenderson, Robt. 53
Wendling, Herman 13
Wentzel, Geo. 53
Wenzel, John 72

Werner, Chas. A. 30
Wesince, Edgar 39
Wessell, Wm. 63
West, Chas. R. 77
West, Wm. 11
West, Frank 39
West, Frank H. 33
West, Perry 52
West, Wm. H. 79
Westernhagen, Adolf von
                42
Weston, Chas. E. 17
Wetzel, Adam 30
Weyworth, Henry 74
Whalen, Jos. 17
Whaler, Thos. C. 75
WHEELAN, JAMES N. 4,15
Wheeler, Jas. W. 59
Whelan, Jas. 86
Whelan, Richard M. 85
Wherstedt, Wm. 16
Whipple, Edward M. 43
Whisten, John 40
Whitback, Leonard B. 53
Whitcomb, Joel R. 39
White, Edward 58
White, E. G. 63
White, Geo. 59
White, Geo. 72
White, Geo. E. 49
White, Jas. 43
White, Jas. 84
White, Jonathan 54
White, Jos. 51
White, Richard H. 80
White, Thos. 15
White, Thos. H. 69
White, Wm. H. 14
Whitford, John 20
Whiting, Chas. 62
Whitlow, Wm. 38
Whitney, Frank 16
WHITTEN, JAMES A. 47,53
Whytenfield, Albert 27
Widmayer, Ferdinand 40
Widmer, Jacob 59
Wiedman, Chas. G. 40
Wieland, Chas. W. 45
Wielenburg, Henry 75
Wierson, Leon W. 64
Wiggins, Thos. J. 85
Wiggins, Wm. H. 22
Wight, Edwin B. 30
Wilbur, Francis A. 73

W

Wilday, Geo. C. 59
Wilhight, Jas. 12
Wilkins, Henry 17
Wilkins, Henry 33
Wilkinson, Thos. 12
Wilkinson, Thos. W.64
Williams, Benj. F. 89
Williams, Chas. 40
Williams, Chas. N.E.
                76
Williams, Edward 17
Williams, Edward 83
Williams, Geo. 74
Williams, Geo. 58
Williams, Geo. A. 69
WILLIAMS, JOHN W.(Dr.)
                2
Williams, Robt. F. 5
Williams, Thos. 59
Williams, Wm. C. 36
Williams, Wm. H. 69
Williamson, John 2
Williamson, Pasavan 35
Wilmer, Louis 79
Wilson, Chas. 52
Wilson, Chas. 65
Wilson, Chas. W. 87
Wilson, Geo. A. 38
Wilson, Geo. W. 52
Wilson, Jas. 48
Wilson, Jas. 69
Wilson, Jas. E. 1,5
Wilson, Jos. 69
Wilson, Milden H. 12
WILSON, ROBERT R. 56
Wilson, Tnos. H. 12
Wilson, Wm. 17
Wilson, Wm. 46
Wilson, Wm. 73
Wilson, Wm. J. 13
Wilton, John H. 59
Windfuhr, Oswald 41
Windolph, Chas. C. 36
Winegardner, Peter 88
Winfield, Herbert 41
Wing, Albert S. 50
Wingfield, Thos. 71
Winkle, John 17
Winn, Rudolph 80
Winn, Jas. 23
Winter, Chas. 48
Wintermute, Chas. 67
Winters, David H. 17

Winters, Fred. 73
Winters, Wm. H. 60
Wiseman, Galen R.
                59
Withrow, Geo. 18
Witmer, Herbert 68
Witt, Henry 38
Witt, John F. A.69
Witzemann, Chas.
                73
Wolchert, Wm. 9
Wolf, Frank 11
Wolfe, Geo. A. 12
Wolfe, Luther B.86
Wolfe, Wm. E. 84
Woller, Jas. 60
Woltering, Francis
                77
Wood, Edwin D. 73
Wood, Geo. 84
Wood, Geo. W. 10
Wood, Jas. 72
Wood, Wm. 88
Woodard, Geo. F.11
WOODBRIDGE, FRANCIS
                8
Woodhouse, Wm. H.11
WOODRUFF, CHAS. A.
                5,7,13
WOODRUFF, THOS. M.
                47,48
Woods, Aaron 30
Woods, Geo. 58
Woods, John 58
WOODSON, ALBERT E.
                55,64
Woodwell, Alford G.
                90
Woollen, Samuel H.
                87
Wordy, Edward 57
Worthy, Even S. 76
Worwood, Chas. H.45
Wray, John 67
Wray, Peter H. 64
Wright, Robt. 64
Wrisley, Jos. S. 87
Wright, Wm. 10
Wyley, Alex. 25
Wylie, Geo. W. 32
Wynn, Jas. 32
Wynkoop, Samuel C.
                87

Y

Yates, Alex. 80
Yearsley, Geo. 61
YEATMAN, RICHARD T.
                82,92
Yeoman, Eurose F. 59
Youk, Johan 14
YOUNG, GEORGE S. 10
Young, Henry 6
Young, Manuel 48
Young, Patrick 60
Young, Peter 6
Young, Robt. H. 55
Young, Wade H. 17
Young, (packer)

Z

Zandt, Chas. 51
Zimmer, Chas. 33
Zimmerman, Albert 86
Zimmerman, Geo. 39
Zimmerman, John K. 92
Zinzer, Louis 74
Ziltle, Conrad 91
Zurmehly, Wilson 88
Zysset, Rudolph 87

2